Bridget Sweeney

The OLD TESTAMENT

The OLD TESTAMENT

God's Word to His People

Rev. James A. Black

Ave María Press • Notre Dame, Ind. 46556

Nihil Obstat:
　　Rev. Robert Hofstetter
　　Censor Librorum

Imprimatur:
　　Most Rev. James D. Niedergeses
　　Bishop of Nashville
　　Feast of All Saints, 1981

© 1982 by Ave Maria Press, Notre Dame, Indiana 46556
All rights reserved.

Library of Congress Catalog Card Number: 82-70087
International Standard Book Number: 0-87793-248-4

Photography:
　　Gary Boyd, 152; Joseph De Caro, 23, 76; Richard N. Clapper, 120; Paul Conklin, 86, 148, 157; Rose Farkas, 107; John E. Fitzgerald, 114; Israeli Tourist Bureau, 17, 94; Robert Maust, 42, 134, 140; Religious News Service, 48; Paul M. Schrock, cover, 36, 82; Russell A. Thompson, 28; Vannucci Foto-Services, 127; Jim Whitmer, 102; Betty Hurwich-Zoss, 54, 70.

Art: Betsy French
Manufactured in the United States of America.

For Don.

Acknowledgments

No book is the final product of any one person. I wish to express my gratitude to Father Owen Campion and the REGISTER staff for a forum for my writing, and for their continued support.

Thanks also to Mary Fran Hayes, of the Audiovisual Department of the Diocese of Nashville, for her assistance in the tracking down of many useful filmstrips and tapes.

A special thanks goes to Sister Mary Rose Bumpus, R.S.M., Mrs. Marguerite Anderson, Miss Mary Ellen Landolina, and Mr. J. Patrick Langdon, all of whom read the manuscript and made many significant suggestions. Thanks also to my brother Don for his invaluable assistance, and to Frank Cunningham, Editor of Ave Maria Press, for his patience and good humor.

Finally, I want to thank the administration, the faculty, and the students of Father Ryan High School in Nashville, Tennessee. It is the faith of this community that has sustained me in many difficult moments. They have taught me much more than I could ever teach them; it is to them that this book is dedicated.

Rev. James A. Black
Feast of All Saints, 1981

Contents

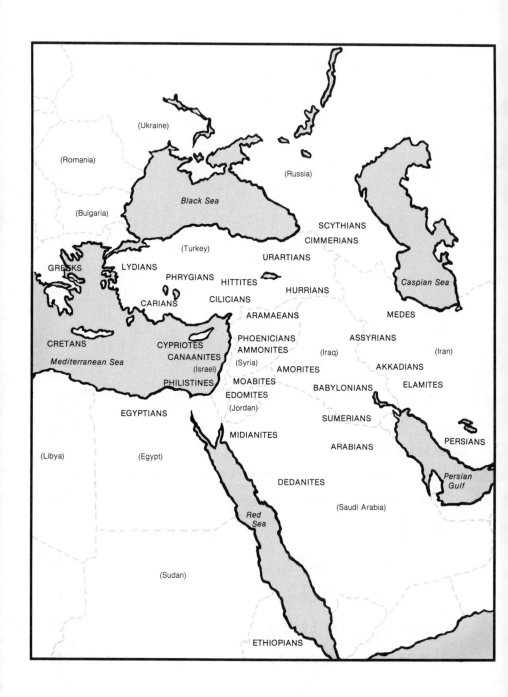

1
An Introduction to the Old Testament

The Bible is different from any book that you have ever read. It comes from a land and a culture different from our own, the Hebrews, and from a time long ago. To best understand the Bible we have to decide just what it really is, and then study a brief amount of background material.

Most people would probably agree that, in some sense, the Bible is the "word of God." But what exactly does that mean? How did the Bible come about? How was it passed down from one generation to the next? What is its message and meaning for us today?

We may find that some of the answers to these questions are not what we expect. However, our investigation will lead us to a fuller understanding of the Old Testament.

Many people have different ideas about the Bible. Some claim that because it's a "holy book," every single word is totally and historically accurate. They refuse to question anything the Bible says, believing that to do so would cast doubt on the Bible as the "word of God."

Others see the Bible as a book of truth, using it to "prove," to their own satisfaction at least, some point of view that they hold. Actually, the Bible is far more important than that.

The Bible isn't a "proof-text"; that is, we can't just pick out isolated quotations that will support a given position or point of view. The writers of the Bible were trying to share their faith; they weren't trying to provide proof for later doctrines or beliefs.

So what is this book called the Bible? It is essentially a sharing of faith—the record of a whole nation's belief in God. The people who wrote the Bible believed that God really did intervene in human history, and that he really does care about creation.

Primarily, then, the Bible is a book of religious truth. Notice the word *religious* in that statement, since it's critical to our understanding of the meaning of the Old Testament. It's not that other forms of truth are deliberately excluded. To the writers of the Bible, other forms just weren't as important. They could understand God only as a God who was involved in his creation, the very cause of everything that happened.

We live in a scientific age, and we have lots of explanations available to us that the ancient Hebrews didn't have. We all know that there is an accepted scientific explanation for rain, but the authors of the Old Testament didn't, and saw God as the immediate cause. They didn't worry about scientific explanations because they didn't have them. Their view of the world around them was quite different from ours in that it was much simpler: They believed God was responsible for everything.

DISCUSSION:

Nearly everyone has seen photographs of the earth taken from space. Ours is the first generation ever to see such a sight. For the first time in human history, we have actually stepped off our planet .and looked back at it from a distance.

Our view of the world is quite scientific and rather complex. The world envisioned by the ancient Hebrews was much simpler. Instead of looking for scientific "cause and effect," as we do today, the Hebrews saw God as the direct cause for everything that happened.

Can you reconcile these two viewpoints?

Most people have tried to read the Bible at one time or another. It takes a lot of effort. If you ever tried, you probably began by reading the Book of Genesis and the story of creation on the first page of your bible. Perhaps you then read of the life of Abraham and the other patriarchs. After that came the Exodus from Egypt and the wanderings of the people in the desert. Up to this point, the reading was fairly interesting because it had action, conflict, suspense, and other appealing characteristics.

But then the story began to slow down. The books of Leviticus, Numbers, and Deuteronomy recited the legal code: law after endless law! You probably tried to read the material because you were always told that it was important, and found much of the material rather boring. As a result, you might have finally given up, saying, "Well, I tried. I really did! This is just too difficult, and I'm not going to read any more because I just don't understand it." After all, you could always claim that you really tried to read the Bible, but just couldn't get through it.

A few people actually go on and read the whole book from cover to cover. They might read the books of Kings, and then read the Chronicles, perhaps not even realizing that many times they're reading identical material. They find two separate accounts of the Ten Commandments, or they find similar passages in different books. Surely, such people must wonder what's going on here.

Few of the sections of the Bible were written at the same time.

Few sections were written for the same reasons. Perhaps we shouldn't read the Bible all at the same time or in the same way. Some of the books are more meaningful than others, and each must be read in its proper context.

As mentioned earlier, the Bible came from a culture quite different from our own, and from a historical context far different from that of today. We can't go back physically in time to those days, but at least we can imagine doing so. The more we can "transport" ourselves back into the time and the culture of the biblical world, the more likely we are to understand what the authors were trying to say. Incidentally, the authors of the Bible were writing to the people of their own time. It's quite unlikely that they ever had us in mind.

The Bible should not be read quickly. To do so is to treat it as an ordinary book, which it isn't. It must be read *slowly, prayerfully, studiously, and reflectively.* And that is what we are going to do. We will not read the entire Old Testament, but we will read quite a bit of it.

In the remainder of the first chapter, we'll look at some further background material. After that, we'll begin our study of the text of the Old Testament itself.

QUESTIONS:

Divide the class into groups of five or six students each, and discuss the following questions:

1) Have you ever tried to read the Bible? All at once or a bit at a time? Did you find it difficult?

2) If so, what were some of the problems you experienced?

3) Try to imagine how the Bible was composed and how it might have gotten here. What factors and elements were involved in its formation?

Share your findings with the class. Which group had the most imaginative explanation for the formation of the Bible?

HOW DID THE BIBLE GET HERE?

The bible that you own came to you in its complete form. It included all the accepted (or "canonical") books, was neatly printed and bound, and was ready to read. As such, it doesn't tell us much about the history involved in its formation.

The ancient culture of the Hebrews, in which the Bible was formed, was one of the spoken rather than the written word. Most people then simply didn't know how to read or write. Their society was fairly simple, and to read or write wasn't really necessary.

The Hebrews believed that they had experienced God and his saving presence in their lives, and they wanted their descendants to understand and appreciate this. They told stories to their children of God's great saving activity in their lives, and what he had done for their nation. Then they passed these stories down from one generation to the next by *word of mouth*. As time passed, certain details in the stories were changed, added, or even lost, but the basic message of the story was still there. Eventually, these fragments were written down as a collection of stories.

DISCUSSION:

Oral tradition is still prevalent in some societies and can be surprisingly accurate. Many people in the Central Pacific—the Caroline Islands and the Gilberts—can still navigate the open ocean using techniques passed down for generations by word of mouth.

Long ago, these people composed songs containing the elements of their navigation system. By chanting these songs as they voyaged throughout the Central and South Pacific, they would know which stars to observe and follow, and what to look for in the swells of the ocean.

Recently, some of these ancient sea routes were retraced using only the oral tradition of navigation that had been passed down by the islanders. The results were amazingly accurate, even by today's standards. Such an experiment suggests the likelihood that much of the oral tradition behind the stories in the Bible is accurate as well.

EXERCISE:

Try gathering some of the oral tradition of your own family. Ask your parents and grandparents about your family history. Where did your ancestors come from and when did they come here? How far back can you trace your family story on the basis of the spoken word? What can you conclude about oral tradition in our society?

Gradually, people collected these various written accounts and put them into an order that achieved a sort of chronology over the years, and the Bible, as we know it, was born. Putting order into these accounts was called "editing." These three stages of development—oral, written, and edited—have no definitive lines between them. At times, all three stages were going on simultaneously throughout the ancient world.

In A.D. 90 in the town of Jamnia in Israel, Jewish leaders met to decide their fate after the fall of Jerusalem. They began considering which books should be accepted into their canon (list) of Scripture. In accord with their traditions and beliefs, the Jews decided over a period of time to include a lesser number of books than the Christians listed as their Old Testament. Christians had already begun to form their own canon by this time, based primarily upon the traditional acceptance of certain books.

This explains one of the several differences between a Protestant version and a Catholic version of the Bible. The most obvious one is that the Catholic version contains more books than the Protestant version. These additional books are called deuterocanonical.

This difference goes back to the period of European history known as the Renaissance, when there was a reawakened interest in and respect for classical antiquity. The idea of translating the Bible from its original languages stems from this period, and, on the surface, it seemed a good idea. But when this was done, the Protestant groups went back to the decisions made by the Jews at Jamnia with regard to which books were in the Old Testament and which were not. The Protestants followed the Jewish canon. The Catholic Church, on the other hand, retained the longer canon which predated the decisions at Jamnia. To this day, the Catholic canon of Scripture is longer than that of its Protestant counterparts.

The Old Testament of the Bible was written in the language of the people who believed that they had experienced God; that is, Hebrew. Translations soon followed, especially into Greek and Latin. The entire Bible was later translated into other languages. Today, the Bible is available in virtually any language.

THINGS TO DO:

1. Compare the Old Testament of a Protestant Bible with the Old Testament of a Catholic Bible. Make a list of the differences.

2. What type of bible do you have at home? at school? What different texts and versions can be found in your school library? Why do you suppose there are so many different versions of the Bible?

THE BIBLE AND FAITH

Since the Bible is a book of faith, it's important that we understand what that means. Faith is not quite the same as

N.B.

knowledge—knowledge comes to us through our senses. Knowledge is what we can learn, either by ourselves or from others, from our senses—sight, hearing, touch, taste, and smell. We know something because we experience it.

Experience is important. We know that ice is cold because we have felt it. We know that the sky is blue because we have seen it. How would we describe that same sky, however, to anyone who had been born blind? That person would never have seen the color, and could not know what the sky actually looked like. We can know because we can perceive.

But what happens when our questions penetrate beyond the realm of our senses? How do we go about finding out information that cannot be experienced by observation? One of humanity's unique abilities is the ability to ask questions. As we pass through different levels of awareness during our lifetime, we begin to question ourselves about the world beyond our senses. We might wonder about such profound issues as why we are here on earth. What is our purpose in life—where are we going? What will happen to us when our body dies?

These questions cannot be answered by using only the data gathered by our senses because no physical data is to be had in these areas. Still, these questions unsettle us throughout our lives, and they must be answered to some degree of satisfaction for our own peace of mind.

It is here that faith enters. If knowledge is based primarily upon information gathered from the senses, then faith (in its simplest form, at least) is belief in something based upon the word of someone else. Put simply, we believe because someone of trust told us so.

Much of life is based upon some type of belief—even unconscious belief. We trust others in many ways. Every time we cross a busy street, we place our faith in the ability of drivers and the mechanical condition of their vehicles. Whenever we enter a building, we trust in the abilities of the architect, the contractor, and their building crews. We never wonder whether or not the building will collapse on us; we simply accept the fact that it will not. We have to believe some things just to get through our everyday existence.

In our human relationships we develop friendships, partnerships, and other manifestations of trust and belief. People who are "as good as their word" tell us a lot about the phenomenon of belief in our daily lives.

It should be noted, though, that belief doesn't always imply total acceptance of a statement. Often, it is the idea itself which is believed rather than the specific language used to express it. We have to get behind the language to the idea it conveys.

Many of us make "conscious exaggeration" statements in our daily speech, especially with our friends. Some students often complain that they always have homework. While it's true that teachers assign homework more often than not, they don't "always" assign it. Students don't always do it, for that matter. But the meaning of the statement is found in the idea that the language conveys; it isn't found in the language itself. What many students are telling their teachers is that they want their evening free, unencumbered by demands upon their time.

How many times have you told your parents that you wanted to go somewhere because "everybody" was going, or that you wanted to do something because "everybody" was doing it? By "everyone," you probably meant several of your friends. But you weren't concerned about the words—you were interested in getting a message across: It meant a lot to you to do something. You got the idea across to your parents when you said that everyone was doing it; you used conscious exaggeration to make a point.

This happens in the Bible as well. Some biblical texts will seem strange to us until we get past the language to the ideas behind it. Sometimes, we can get so distracted by unusual descriptions or details in the text that we forget the religious message they were meant to convey. For instance, while many people could probably summarize the tale of Joshua and the battle at Jericho with reasonable accuracy, how many of those same people could say just what the religious message behind that story is—that is, that God was with his people? We have to remember that we're not reading the Old Testament as a historical narrative of ancient times. Rather, we're looking for the religious message that it contains, the message that often lies hidden in its prose. After all, isn't that message the specific reason why the Bible was written in the first place?

EXERCISE:

1. What "conscious exaggeration" words and phrases do you use in conversation at school or at home? Compare your list with others.

2. Look carefully at the list you have made. Can you explain or identify the specific idea behind the "conscious exaggeration" statements you used?

3. How many situations in your life can you identify where faith of any kind is involved? Include everyday situations.

THE BIBLE, INSPIRATION, AND INERRANCY

An obvious difference between the Bible and any other book lies in the claim that many people make for it: The Bible is the word of God. But when these same people are asked what that means, many of them are unable to give a satisfactory answer. Two generally accepted biblical characteristics that we will investigate next are *inspiration* and *inerrancy*.

When many people hear the word *inspiration* they believe that it means they are being challenged to a better life by the words, actions, or example of another. They are inspired to live a certain type of life. That's not what is meant by biblical inspiration because many other books besides the Bible produce this result, yet none claims that it is the word of God.

Or, people imagine biblical inspiration as something that takes place when God or an angel whispers words into the ear of the authors of the Bible, and tells them what they should write down. That's not inspiration either—that's note-taking (the same thing you probably do in class). Hardly inspiring!

Inspiration, in its proper sense, is what theologians call a "mystery," something that cannot be fully explained. But even if we cannot totally define inspiration, at least we can describe what it is in a general way.

The authors who composed various sections of the Bible could have been unaware that what they wrote was God's word. The author just happened to say something that God wanted said. The author wrote, unaware that there was a deeper level to his communication. God utilized the author to get his religious message across to people, and thus the message probably had a far more important meaning than the one the author wrote consciously.

Inspiration is concerned with only one area: religious truth. It doesn't matter whether or not the sacred authors realized that inspiration was taking place; they didn't have to know about it for it to happen.

Regarding inspiration, Pope Pius XII said in his 1943 encyclical, *Divino Afflante Spiritu:*

> No one who has a proper idea of biblical inspiration will be surprised to find that the sacred writers, like other men of antiquity, employed certain techniques of exposition and narrative, certain idioms characteristic of the Semitic language, certain exaggerated, often paradoxical expressions designed for the sake of emphasis.

Inspiration is a complex topic. Again, it is basically a matter of God getting a religious message across to people in terms they can understand. One of the proofs of God's love for us is that he communicates with us in a way that is intelligible to us.

All the books of the Bible are inspired, but that doesn't mean that the Bible contains no mistakes. When we speak of the Bible's lack of mistakes, we're talking about inerrancy.

Inerrancy refers to the fact that there are no mistakes in the religious truth that God wants to reveal to us. Please note the words "religious truth." The Bible says what God wants it to say. It makes no mistakes in terms of what God wants us to know.

But that's not a guarantee against other inaccuracies. When talking about statements other than religious truth, and in using human language to do so, the Bible can be inaccurate.

We can search the Scriptures and find many statements which modern science would contradict. We might find several historical inaccuracies. After all, we're dealing with human authors as well as with divine inspiration. And, as long as we're dealing with humans, we're dealing with the possibility of mistakes.

We have to listen to what the biblical authors have to say about God in their own way. We can't impose later ideas or understandings or insights upon people who didn't have them. The Bible is a book of religious belief, and it must be taken as such. In that sense, it contains no mistakes.

QUESTIONS:

1. How do you think God communicated with people in Old Testament times?

2. Does God communicate with people today? In what ways?

APPROACHES TO THE BIBLE

The way we approach the Bible will very much determine the way we will read it, and thus the degree to which we understand it. The background that we bring to the Scriptures will also color our understanding of what we read. Let's look at a few common approaches to the Bible—some of them erroneous—since this will give us a better understanding of how to read and interpret it.

1. The Fundamental Approach

A popular approach today is the fundamental, or literal, approach to the Bible. Those who adhere to this view insist on taking every phrase, description, and text of the Bible literally; that is, word for word as they appear in the text. This approach often gains favor when a society increases in complexity; people tend to look for easy solutions to difficult problems. Possibly, this approach misunderstands the concept of "word of God." Certainly, this approach creates more problems than it solves.

Those who take the Bible absolutely literally often fail to take into account the changes that language undergoes through usage. For example, the word "nice" has generally pleasant connotations to us today, but in the Middle English usage (the 12th to the 15th centuries) it meant "foolish." Today, one can certainly be happy and carefree, but to be "gay" puts one into altogether different company. Words can develop new meanings; language changes. Besides, the *idea* to be communicated is more important than the words chosen to express it.

Beyond the language problems of the fundamental approach is the additional problem of simple logic. For example, in the first creation account in the Book of Genesis (there are actually two such accounts in the opening chapters of the book), we read that God created the light and separated it from the darkness on the first day. Yet it was not until the fourth day that the sun, moon, and stars—our light sources—were created. Now, unless we are to separate philosophically our concept of light from our concept of source (an unlikely situation for an unsophisticated Hebrew author) we can see the obvious problems. Besides, did you ever wonder who was present to take notes on all this, if we are to follow the account literally?

Back in the 1940s, Pope Pius XII condemned fundamentalism as a refusal to understand the Scriptures. The approach is not without its value, of course, insofar as something can be gained from any form of bible reading. However, it is likely that people using this approach will limit rather seriously their depth of understanding of the Scriptures, and may end up with more questions than answers.

2. *The Scientific Approach*

The second approach to be considered is called the scientific approach, for want of a better name. Actually, this isn't really an approach to the study of Scripture at all, but rather, an approach to one's view of life and environment. In simple terms, this view would say that whenever science and the Bible contradict one another, preference is to be given to the scientific explanation. The obvious problem here, however, is that an investigation of the meaning of the scriptural passage in question is ignored.

This approach sets up an unfair comparison between two different studies, like comparing apples and oranges. Besides, discarding a biblical view in favor of a scientific approach eliminates some of the biblical problems, but it does nothing to solve them. Using our creation example again, this approach would reject the account in the Bible. But it would never seek to understand what the account in the Bible was saying.

3. The Concordist Approach

The concordist approach attempts to harmonize the first two views. Using the same example as before, proponents of this approach might suggest that a biblical day of creation was thousands of years long, attempting to reconcile the biblical account of creation with that of science, which claims that creation took millions of years.

If the days were thousands of years long back then, surely there would be evidence. Besides, if we have found the first two approaches inadequate, it seems logical to assume that a combination of those two approaches would be inadequate also.

4. The Critical Approach

The fourth approach is called the critical approach. In essence, it's an attempt to take the Bible on its own terms instead of ours. Those who use the critical approach try to get behind the written records. They attempt to study the politics, cultures, and circumstances surrounding the formation of a biblical account. They try to discern the many oral traditions that predate the written account, and how the various strands of tradition were woven together and edited into a section of a biblical story.

Those who wrote the Bible thought of their readers as people of their own time and culture. It's not realistic to presume that they thought of the habits and customs of the people who would come along from two to four thousand years later. Those who utilize the critical approach try to determine what the biblical authors were saying to the people of their own time. If we can find out what that message was, we will have a better chance of understanding how that message applies to our own situation today. This is the approach endorsed by the Catholic Church, and it is the approach that is used in this book.

DISCUSSION:

What approach to the Bible did you take? Why? Survey the class to see which approach was most common.

THE BIBLE AND SPECIAL TECHNIQUES

As many different authors wrote down sections of the Bible over the years, they used many methods of storytelling that were familiar to their people. Because the Bible comes from a foreign culture a few thousand years removed from our own, we need to look at some of these literary techniques so we can understand just what the authors were trying to say, and why they said it.

1. *Etiology*

One such literary technique is called etiology. A practical description of etiology is *an explanation after the fact to explain an already existing situation.* Someone may have discovered an interesting or unusual situation, and then simply invented a story of its origin, perhaps using a fanciful explanation. It's a legitimate literary device that has been used in many cultures, even in our own day. Its purpose is not to fool people, but rather to provide a "folk explanation" for a given situation.

Suppose, for example, you had noticed there are a great number of lakes in northern Minnesota and Wisconsin. A natural explanation for this fact would be that at one time a large amount of glacial ice covered the area. When it retreated northward, it scraped away the earth and left large depressions that eventually filled up with water. These are the lakes that we see today.

A good example of an etiology here would go like this: "Once upon a time there was a giant of a man named Paul Bunyan who had a huge blue ox named Babe. As Babe trampled around in the north woods, she left her footprints behind. These eventually filled with water, becoming the lakes of this particular area today."

Again, this explanation isn't really a deliberate attempt to trick anyone. It takes an existing fact—the many lakes in the area—and gives a fanciful explanation for their origin. Certain phrases in the English translations of the Bible will sometimes tip you off to the presence of an etiology. You might read something like this: "And that is why (such and such a thing) happens, down to the present day." Such a phrase often indicates the presence of an etiological account.

It may upset us a bit to read passages we formerly took as fact and now consider etiological. But that's not really the issue. The point is to find the *religious message* of the accounts, and not to spend our time or energy worrying about whether or not we're dealing with factual history. Let's leave that to the biblical scholars. The issue for us is the theology of the account—the religious message.

A good example of a biblical etiology is the story relating the origin of the Moabites and the Ammonites. It's found in the Book of Genesis at the end of chapter 19 (see 19:30-38). In the story, Lot's daughters got him inebriated and then had relations with him. Both became pregnant, and both bore sons: one was named Moab, and the other Ammon. According to the story, these were the dishonorable origins of the ancestors of the Moabites and the Ammonites, two tribes that the Hebrews didn't get along with.

No one seriously holds that this story presents a factual historical account. But let's look at it etiologically. The circumstances during the time of its writing were that the Hebrews, for a number of reasons, had little use for the Moabites and the Ammonites. They had to justify their ill feelings toward these tribes, so they provided a folk story about their origins. Calling into question someone's ancestry is hardly an unusual way to "put down" other people, even today. But the story shows how an etiology works. It's an explanation after the fact to explain an already existing situation; in this case, the inability of the Hebrews, the Moabites, and the Ammonites to get along with each other.

2. *Symbolic Numbers*

A second type of literary device is the use of symbolic numbers. In many instances in both the Old and the New Testaments we find various numbers mentioned with surprising frequency. These numbers had specific meanings, and were not meant to be taken literally. Such symbolic numbers were a phenomenon common to many cultures of the ancient world, and even occur in some cultures today.

Some numbers were considered more sacred or important than others. One of the most common was the number seven. It signified perfection, completion, holiness; this was the most important Hebrew sacred number. Twelve, likewise, had a holy significance, and 40 days represented a long time. Forty years stood for one generation in a culture whose life span was considerably shorter than ours.

Multiples of these numbers were also used. In one of the gospel accounts, Jesus was asked how often we are to forgive our brother when he wrongs us. Jesus responded, "Not seven times, but seventy times seven times." Thus, we are to forgive completely, infinitely, perfectly—not just a specific number of times.

When we read of the Hebrews' wandering in the desert for 40 years, we now realize that the biblical authors were referring to the approximate length of time it would take for one generation to die out and for another to replace it. It didn't necessarily mean 40 years of 365 days each.

It is important for us to be aware of such literary techniques; indeed, to be aware of all the introductory material we have covered so far, as we begin our study of the Old Testament. Such material will aid us in our understanding of the times and the circumstances of the writing of the Bible. This, in turn, can only give us a better insight into what the biblical authors were saying to their own people, and ultimately, to us.

EXERCISE:

1) Look up the following passages in your bible:

Genesis 11: 1-9 (The Tower of Babel)
Genesis 32: 23-33 (Jacob and the Angel)

Why are these passages considered etiological?

2) In reading the Book of Genesis find two more stories that are etiological. Why are they considered as such? What is the religious theme of each story?

CHAPTER SUMMARY:

1. The Bible is a book of religious truth.

2. It's much easier to read and understand the Old Testament if we understand the context in which it was formed.

3. The Bible began with oral tradition—stories passed down by word of mouth from generation to generation.

4. Historical circumstances caused these oral traditions to be written down and gathered together.

5. We have to go beyond the words of a statement to discover the idea those words attempt to convey.

6. *Religiously* speaking, the Bible says what God wants it to say, and it makes no errors in doing so.

7. The critical approach to the Old Testament examines the politics, the culture, and the religious ideas surrounding the formation of a biblical account so that we might better understand its meaning.

8. Etiologies and symbolic numbers are only two of the many devices the authors of the Old Testament used to convey their message.

CHAPTER ONE IN REVIEW:

1. What does it mean when we say that the Bible is the "word of God"?

2. Is the Bible a record of God's activity, or a record of man's response to that activity?

3. Why should I read the Bible at all?

4. If the formation of the Bible was so involved and complicated, how do we know that it's accurate?

5. What is meant by "religious truth"?

6. Why can't I claim that the Bible means whatever I say it means?

7. Who really wrote the Bible: God or man or both?

8. What are some of the problems to be found in reading the Bible word for word?

9. Do various literary techniques change the truth of the Bible if the Bible is concerned only with religious truth? Why/why not?

TERMS TO KNOW:

Bible	oral tradition	written tradition
edited tradition	chronology	faith
deuterocanonical	inspiration	inerrancy
mystery	fundamental approach	scientific approach
concordist approach	critical approach	etiology
symbolic numbers	conscious exaggeration	

SPECIAL PROJECT:

Go to the school library and find a biblical dictionary and a biblical commentary. Look up the explanations for *texts and versions, inspiration,* and *inerrancy.* Report on your findings to the class.

2
The Pentateuch

With the necessary introductory material now behind us, we have a better possibility of understanding the Old Testament. What will follow is not a biblical commentary, but a guide for the student who reads the Old Testament to discover its story line. We'll begin with the first part of the Old Testament, which is called the Pentateuch. "Pentateuch" comes from a Greek word, *penta,* meaning *five;* thus, the Pentateuch is made up of the first five books of the Bible.

Traditionally, the authorship of the Pentateuch is ascribed to Moses, but it is authorship in a much broader sense than we are accustomed to today. In our culture, only the person who writes is considered an author. In the Hebrew understanding, however, both the person who penned the work and the person who originally preached the material could be considered the authors. In that sense, we can say that Moses "stood behind" the Pentateuch and was its author.

The first book of the Pentateuch is the Book of Genesis. We'll start our investigation of God's plan in the Old Testament with Genesis 12 rather than Genesis 1; the first 11 chapters of the book form a small narrative in itself, and come from a later date. We'll look at some of that material later. For now, our concern is with the main story line of the Old Testament, the description of God's saving activity.

At the beginning of each biblical book that you will study, you will find specific material that must be read. These selections are minimal, but essential to understanding the Old Testament. No summary or commentary can substitute for reading the Bible. Of course, you're free to read more than the minimal reading, and this is strongly encouraged. Your teacher may assign additional reading. The key idea gives you an indication of the main point of the reading.

GENESIS

Reading: Genesis 12, 15.

Key Idea: The promise from God to Abraham.

Since our primary interest in the Old Testament is the relationship between God and his people, we begin our study where that relationship is formed: Genesis 12. The chapter begins with God's intervention into human history. Abram, we are told, was "called" by God. Whether God simply appeared to him, let his will be known through a dream, or whatever, we just don't know. After all, we're not particularly interested in *how* God did something; we're interested in *what* he did. If we can keep this idea fixed in our minds as we study the Old Testament, the meaning behind the Scriptures will become clearer to us. Somehow, God told Abram to leave the city of Ur, his hometown in the land of the Chaldeans, and go to the land that God would show him. And this is what Abram did.

The Covenant

In chapter 15, God formed a "covenant" with Abram. A covenant is a commitment between two people to do something for each other. A covenant differs from a contract in that a covenant is based upon love, whereas a contract is based upon legal obligation. It's interesting to note that a covenant is usually made between equal parties. Obviously, when God made a covenant with Abram, this was not to say that Abram was God's equal. Rather, God chose to work in ways that human beings could understand.

The covenant God made with Abram in chapter 15 is actually an outline for the entire Bible. Thus, it's rather important at the outset that we understand the meaning of the covenant. It has three parts. God told Abram that:

a) Abram would be the father of a nation;

b) this nation would have a land of its own; and

c) through this land and through this nation, all nations of the earth would find blessing.

By its very nature, a covenant is based upon the faith and trust of one person in the other. Thus, in response to the provisions of this covenant, Abram was required to be willing to trust in God.

The Patriarchs

When we read further in the Book of Genesis, we find that Abram (later, Abraham) did indeed become the father of a nation. He married a woman named Sarah, but initially they were unable to have children. Abraham did father a child (Ishmael) by Sarah's slave. But because the slave was merely considered Sarah's property, the relationship was not as binding as it would have been if he had a son through Sarah. Finally, through the intervention of the Lord, Abraham and Sarah had a son whom they named Isaac.

Isaac grew up, married, and had a son named Jacob, who later became a leader of his tribe. It was Jacob who raised up 12 sons who ultimately became the ancestors of the 12 tribes of Israel. Thus, the first part of the covenant between God and Abraham was brought to fulfillment within the span of three generations; Abraham had become the father of a nation.

Toward the end of the Book of Genesis, we read of the life of one of Jacob's 12 sons, Joseph. Joseph was sold by his brothers into slavery in Egypt because of their jealousy. Once in Egypt, Joseph managed to acquire prominence and power. When a famine arose, affecting all the ancient Near East, Joseph and the Egyptians were in a position to invite the Hebrews to live in northeast Egypt (an area called Goshen) where there was relatively good land for their flocks and sufficient food for the people. This set the stage for the next book of the Pentateuch, Exodus, in which the Hebrews became enslaved and had to escape from the land of Egypt.

DISCUSSION:

1) Have you ever tried to make a "family tree"? Why does it seem so important to people to know their ancestry?

2) We have seen that a covenant is a relationship based on love and a contract is an agreement based on law:

> Under what circumstances is a marriage a covenant? A contract? Is one likely to be more enduring than the other? Explain.

Make a list of other covenants in your family, your church, your school, or among your friends.

Immortality in the Old Testament

Why do you suppose it was so important for Abraham to have a son? Actually, it had a great deal to do with the Hebrew understanding of immortality at this point in Old Testament history. Our perception of life after death today differs greatly from the one in this period of the Old Testament. The ancient Hebrews had little to hope for after death: no promise of heaven, no eternal life—a rather bleak future.

Many believed that a person lived on primarily through his sons. Obviously, then, it was important for a Hebrew to have sons to follow him. And, quite logically, Abraham could hardly have become the father of a nation if he were not first the father of a family (thus, the importance of his son Isaac over that of Ishmael). A person also lived on after death through the community's remembrance of his good deeds. Somehow, as long as the community's memory of a man did not perish, he did not perish.

Our awareness of these beliefs will help us understand many Old Testament references. For example, there are many long lists of names in the Bible. This was at least a type of immortality for some of the people: a "living on" after death in the minds of others. Multiple marriages, the great tragedy of dying childless, and long lists of names all reflect an attempt to preserve some sort of immortality for the people involved.

EXERCISE:

1) How would you choose to be remembered after your death?

    by your family _____

    by your friends _____

    by your community _____

    Why? _____

---

2) In the Apostles' Creed we say "I believe . . . in the resurrection of the body and life everlasting." Write a brief paragraph saying what that statement means to you right now.

3) Make a list of famous persons who are remembered for what they did during their lifetimes. Is this a form of immortality?

4) Can you think of some things people have done throughout history in order to remain immortal?

EXODUS

Reading: Exodus 2:23-25, 3-12, 15-20, 24.

Key Idea: The formation of the People of God.

The Book of Exodus opens with a general summary of the enslavement of the Hebrews and their oppression under the Egyptian pharaohs. Many scholars claim that the people who had known Joseph were people known as the Hyksos who had overthrown the Egyptians many years earlier. They and the Hebrews shared a similar background. The pharaohs who "knew nothing of Joseph" (Ex 1:8) were actually Egyptian pharaohs who enslaved the Hebrews once they were able to drive out the Hyksos.

God and Moses

In chapter 3, God identified himself to Moses by name in the incident of the burning bush. He called himself "Yahweh," which is most often translated as "I am." We find in the chapters immediately following that Moses was reluctant to accept the task that Yahweh had given him. Eventually, he agreed to God's plan for him by appearing before Pharaoh, asking for the release of the Hebrews, and invoking a series of plagues upon the Egyptians when Pharaoh refused to cooperate.

Moses and Pharaoh

Perhaps you've seen the movie, *The Ten Commandments*—a rather dramatic portrayal of this section of the Bible. Even if you have not, this section of the Old Testament is quite interesting to read; in fact, we can become so involved in the story that we overlook the religious message that it conveys. We don't have to be overly concerned with trying to determine exactly what happened historically. To do so, again, is to ask the wrong questions of the Bible. The point is that God was somehow going to save the Hebrews from Egypt and bring them out of that country. All the plagues took place, and eventually with the plague of the death of the first-born, the Hebrews were released; indeed, they were asked to leave the country.

Many scholars believe that the plagues can be explained natural-
ly, and that they occurred over a long period of time. To explain the
plagues in this way hardly diminishes God's power, since (in the
Hebrew mind, at least) God stood behind everything that happened.
If people can explain, 30 or 40 years from now, events that we consider unexplainable today, that certainly doesn't diminish the effects
of those events upon us.

Once the Hebrews left Egypt, they went out into the desert. The
Egyptian leadership had a change of heart and ordered the pursuit of
the Hebrews. This brings us to the account of the crossing of the sea
(Ex 14).

Most people are aware by now that many of the better ancient
texts say "Reed Sea" or "Sea of Reeds" rather than "Red Sea." The
Red Sea, after all, would have been quite some distance out of the
Hebrews' way. The name "Reed Sea" suggests a shallow body of
water, perhaps somewhat marsh-like in appearance. Somehow, the
Hebrews got through and the Egyptians met disaster. We could
speculate at great length as to what happened there, but this, again,
wouldn't serve our purpose. Nor is that why the story was written.
The point is that, somehow, the Hebrews experienced Yahweh as saving them from the Egyptians.

Chapter 15 contains the "Song of Moses," most likely a very ancient poem celebrating the Hebrews' victory over the Egyptians. The
surviving poetry of an ancient culture tends to be older than its prose.
Poetry, with its rhyme, meter, and sometimes even music, was held
more easily in the tribal memory than was prose. Many poetic accounts in the Old Testament, then, are quite ancient. Some scholars
believe that chapter 15 of Exodus, the poetic account of the crossing
of the sea, is one of the oldest existing parts of the entire Bible. In an
age in which reading and writing were uncommon, such a song allowed everyone to know and remember what God had done for
the people.

In subsequent chapters of Exodus, we find the care and concern of the Lord for his people in providing them with food and water while they wandered in the desert. In chapter 19, the people arrived at Mount Sinai.

The Sinai Covenant

The events which occurred at Mount Sinai are really one of the more central issues in the book. It is here that the people were formed into a unified group with a common bond and purpose. At this point, they became the People of God as Yahweh reaffirmed his covenant with them.

After the people arrived at Mount Sinai, their leader Moses went up on the mountain. Note in the text the awesome imagery for the presence of Yahweh: smoke, lightning, thunder, and so on, all suggestive of God's power. In chapter 20, Moses was given the Ten Commandments. These are probably a codification (gathering and ordering) of already existing practices and beliefs of the people. Numbers nine and ten, as we know them, are combined in this narrative.

In chapter 24, the people were required to assent to these commandments, as well as to their elaboration in the intervening chapters. And they did agree:

> We will observe all that Yahweh has
> decreed; we will obey (Ex 24:7).

This was the covenant—God's part and man's part. It could be stated thus: "If you obey my statutes, ordinances, and decrees, then I will be your God, and you shall be my people."

"If . . . then . . ." is the key phrase in a covenant because covenants are built upon conditions. In our examination of the Old Testament, we will come to see that frequently the Hebrews did not obey the commands of the Lord. But they were the ones who broke the covenant. Yahweh was always faithful and constant.

The remainder of the Book of Exodus is somewhat anachronistic; that is, out of its proper time period. It shows the various details of the construction of the Ark of the Covenant, wherein the tablets of the Law would be kept. But the dwelling place for the Ark is a small scale model of the Temple in Jerusalem, which wasn't built until several hundred years later. Of course, the problem is resolved when we realize that the account was written down long after both events had transpired.

The final part of the book is rather tedious for most people, and not terribly relevant for us today. Suffice it to say that, at the end of the book, God manifested his presence to the people by allowing his glory to appear in the dwelling place.

The importance of the Book of Exodus is shown not only by the great deeds and miracles it depicts, but also in the accounts of the formation of the People of God and their deliverance from the Egyptians by Yahweh.

DISCUSSION:

Divide the class into groups of five or six students each. Discuss how the people who were slaves in Egypt were different from the people at Sinai at the end of the Book of Exodus. What happened to them to make them different? What does it mean to be "chosen" by God?

Now try to think of ways that God has had an effect on your life. Did God use everyday, natural circumstances and events? Share your conclusions with the other groups.

DEUTERONOMY

Reading: Deuteronomy 5, 30.

Key Idea: Choose life instead of death.

The title "Deuteronomy" comes from the Greek words *deuteros* (second) and *nomos* (word, law). Thus, the book is the second "giving" of the Law. The book was written in the form of five major speeches given by Moses, and is basically a summation of the laws in the previous books of Leviticus and Numbers. These two books have been omitted, since we find their general summation here.

The Ten Commandments are listed again in chapter 5, and here they vary only slightly from the account in Exodus 20. Here, the ninth and tenth commandments are separated, whereas they were combined in the account in Exodus.

In chapter 6:4, we find the "great commandment" referred to by Jesus in the New Testament. This commandment, called the *Shema,* was the Jewish declaration of monotheism, or belief in one God. This was one belief that set the Hebrews apart from other nations.

> Listen, Israel: Yahweh our God is the one Yahweh. You shall love Yahweh your God with all your heart, with all your soul, with all your strength (Dt 6:4).

Moses and the Law

In this book, and within the framework of the whole legal code, Moses placed an emphasis on the importance of the people's faithfulness to the observance of the Law. He set two choices before the people. One was totally right, and the other was totally wrong. If they followed the Law, the results would be good. If, on the other hand, they chose not to follow the Law, all sorts of tragic events would occur. Moses claimed that it was literally a life-or-death choice, and he urged the people to choose life (follow the Law) so that they might be allowed to enter the Promised Land (Palestine).

At the end of the book, with the Hebrew people on the threshold of the Promised Land, Moses died. When the Hebrews wrote down the story later on, it bothered them that their greatest leader had died before getting into the Promised Land. Remember, they always saw the hand of Yahweh behind everything that happened.

Most probably, Moses simply died before getting into the Promised Land. But the authors wouldn't rest with that simple fact. Some later believed that Moses had died because he had done something wrong, or committed some sin, although the Scriptures are not at all clear on this point. But the explanation of Moses being punished for

some wrongdoing, factual or not, would satisfy their theological sensibilities.

After the death of Moses, a man named Joshua took over the leadership of the People of God. His name, by the way, comes from the same root word as the name "Jesus." It was Joshua who led the people into the Promised Land from the plains of Moab, where they had been waiting.

Why Law?

It would be easy for us to pass over Leviticus, Numbers, and Deuteronomy as sections of Scripture that need not concern us because of their particular interest in Law and religious ritual. Perhaps we should reflect for a moment on the idea behind the laws of the Old Testament, as well as the values they attempted to preserve.

One of the purposes of the law is to enshrine or protect a value. The value, obviously, is more significant than the language used to express it. But to be preserved for and understood by the society, it is expressed in language—it is written down.

The Bible uses two terms to describe law: *spirit of the law* and *letter of the law*. The spirit of the law refers to the idea or value which the law protects. The letter of the law is the specific language of the law itself. Surprisingly it is possible to keep the letter of the law (the language) and violate the spirit of the law (the idea behind it).

For example, there used to be a law in the Catholic Church that we could not eat meat on any Friday. The idea behind the law was for us to do penance for our sins. But many people thoroughly enjoyed seafood and looked forward to Fridays as a change of pace. Was this penance for their sins? Hardly. They kept the letter of the law because they did not eat meat on Friday. But it is doubtful that they kept the spirit of the law, since they were hardly thinking of penance every time they sat down to a seafood dinner.

EXERCISE:

The letter of the law deals with *what* we do. The spirit of the law deals with *why* we do it.

Perhaps we can gain some insight to this by making some judgments on cheating. *Do not cheat* is a rule (law) in school. But what does cheat mean? What is the value behind the law? Check yes or no on the following questions.

1. Last year your brother wrote a term paper for history class. This year you have the same class but with a different teacher. You turn in the same paper with your name on it. Did you "cheat"?   Yes_____   No_____

2. You wrote a paper last year for a class, and now you find that the same topic is appropriate for one of your classes this year. You make a fresh copy of your old paper and turn it in. Did you "cheat"?   Yes_____   No_____

3. You hear a discussion about abortion on a talk show. The next day the same topic comes up in your religion class. You present the arguments you heard on TV. The teacher assumes they are your own thoughts and compliments you because they are so well thought out and timely. You smile and say this is a topic you've thought a lot about. Did you "cheat"?   Yes_____   No_____

4. You are selling your car. You mention to the buyer that the body is rusting in places. You do not mention that the car needs a brake job—and the buyer does not ask about the brakes. Did you "cheat"?   Yes_____   No_____

5. What if the buyer in #4 above did ask you specifically about the brakes—and you said they were O.K.? Did you "cheat"?   Yes_____   No_____

6. You did all your math homework, but accidentally left the paper at home. The teacher will not accept that as an excuse—any paper not turned in the day it's due receives an F. You don't have time to do the work over, but if you hurry through lunch hour you do have time to copy the work from a friend. Remember—you have done the paper

completely on your own already. Is copying your friend's paper "cheating"?   Yes_____   No_____

After you have answered these questions, break up into groups of five or six students and discuss. Do you think "cheat" means exactly the same thing in each of these cases? If you think each case is a form of cheating, are some more serious than others? Why? Why not?

It would be worth your time to look over some of the "legal codes" in the books of Leviticus, Numbers, and Deuteronomy. Try to discover the values that the laws were protecting. It may be that an emphasis on the letter of the law, rather than on the values behind it, led to considerable difficulties for the Hebrews later on. Indeed, it might not be that different for some of us today.

THINGS TO DO:

1) Research some of the religious practices of the people of the area around Palestine in the time of Moses—for example, the Egyptians, Assyrians, Canaanites, Hittites. Was monotheism unusual at that time? Report your findings to the class.

2) List as many individual laws as you can that affect your personal life. Include the rules of your school and home, civil laws and traffic laws. Can you determine the values behind these laws? Share your findings with the class.

CHAPTER SUMMARY:

1. Salvation history began with God's calling of Abraham.

2. A covenant is a commitment of love between two parties.

3. The covenant that God made with Abraham forms an outline of the entire Bible.

4. The early Old Testament view of immortality was quite different from our understanding of immortality today.

5. We must try to identify *what* God did, rather than *how* he did it.

6. In the Book of Exodus, the People of God were joined together in the Sinai Covenant.

7. The Law was an attempt to protect the past experiences and traditions of the Hebrew people.

8. The spirit of the law is the value behind the law. The letter of the law is the language of the law itself.

9. If we are only concerned with keeping the letter of the law, we might not realize the value that the law attempts to protect.

CHAPTER TWO IN REVIEW:

1. When the covenant between God and man was broken time and time again, we see that God re-established it. Why?

2. The word *genesis* means "beginnings." Why is that a suitable title for the book that contains the story of Abraham?

3. Why is the "formation of the People of God" a key idea in the Book of Exodus?

4. Why is there a need for law in religion? in society?

5. How can we best determine the value behind a law?

6. Is your own personal religious outlook legalistic? That is, do I do things because the law says that I have to do them?

TERMS TO KNOW:.

Pentateuch	covenant	patriarch
immortality	Reed Sea	Sinai Covenant
anachronism	Shema	spirit of the law
letter of the law		

SPECIAL PROJECT:

Look up the suggested dates for many of the people in the Pentateuch: Abraham, Isaac, Jacob, Joseph, Moses. Make a chart showing the chronology of the Old Testament. Keep your chart "up to date" throughout the remainder of your Old Testament study.

3
The Historical Books

The first two books that we will consider in this chapter, Joshua and Judges, form a bridge or transition between the Pentateuch and what are often called the historical books. After Joshua and Judges we will then study the historical books.

They are called historical, not so much because they follow our standards of history today, but rather because they show the theological formation of the Hebrew nation over a long period of time. And, insofar as they follow a chronological order, we can say that they are somewhat faithful to history.

JOSHUA

Reading: Joshua 1, 2, 3, 6, 24.

Key Idea: Getting into the Promised Land.

The story of Joshua began in the 12th century B.C., south of the area called the Transjordan. Joshua, Moses' successor as leader of the Hebrew people, had brought the people very close to the Promised Land.

But other nations, already living in the area, were not anxious to have a large tribe migrate through their land. Thus, the main tribal bloc couldn't get through to Palestine directly. The country of Edom blocked their path from the Dead Sea to the Gulf of Aqaba. In response, the Hebrews turned eastward toward the desert. They would have to pass around Edom.

Moab, like Edom, was also in the way, and was too strong to conquer at this time. Later, the Hebrews won a few battles here and began to settle in the area. But they really couldn't keep a foothold. Amorites from the south kept up the fighting and harassed the Hebrews, forcing them to move along again.

The Hebrews defeated two minor kings in this area: Sihon, king of the Amorites, and Og, king of Bashan. Historically, there were a lot of these minor conquests in the Transjordanian area that were simply combined in the biblical accounts over the years. Eventually, the Hebrews worked their way into the Promised Land.

It's interesting that the books of Joshua and Judges depict approximately the same period of time. Joshua gives us a rather broad general overview of the conquest of Palestine. The book seems to indicate that events went favorably for the Hebrews, who conquered their enemies with little difficulty. Judges, on the other hand, shows more specifically how areas of Palestine were subdued, and how it was often done at great cost, if at all. Judges is the far more realistic of the two books, since history testifies to the difficulty of gaining control of Palestine.

In the Book of Joshua, there are many attempts on the part of the author to make Joshua himself another Moses. Like Moses, he was the divinely inspired leader of the people. Like Moses, he conversed with God face to face. As Moses had parted the sea, so Joshua parted the Jordan River in preparation for the crossing over into Palestine.

It's rather curious to note that not all 12 tribes actually wished to enter the Promised Land. When the tribes were in the Transjordan, they found good land, plenty of water and forage for their sheep and goats, and relatively friendly neighbors.

A few of the tribes made an agreement with Moses (and restated it with Joshua) that they would dwell in the Transjordan and would never claim any land in Palestine itself. In return, the men of these tribes promised to march with the rest of the Hebrews in warfare, returning to the Transjordan only when victory belonged to the people. Moses had feared that Reuben, Gad, and the half tribe of Manasseh (the Transjordanian tribes) would not honor their commitment to fight with the rest of the Hebrew nation. At first, these tribes kept their word, but ultimately it became increasingly difficult to get them to help out.

There are so many stories involved in the Book of Joshua, from so many different sources and periods of time, that they are difficult to catalog accurately. However, it is fair to say that the stories in Joshua are simplifications and popular accounts of the events described. But the authors of these stories were trying to convey a uniform message: *The hand of God was with his people in their conquests.* These written accounts contained not only the primitive stories, but also the insights of the later period when the stories were written down.

One of the more disturbing practices of the Hebrews (and other primitive tribes) in ancient times is described in chapter 6:21. With reference to the attack and capture of Jericho, the attacking Hebrews

> . . . burned the town and all within it except the silver and gold and things of bronze and iron; these they put into the treasury of Yahweh's house (Jos 6:24).

This is referred to as the ban, or *herem,* and was originally a dedication of everything to God. When a city was captured and placed under the *herem,* everything was divided into two classifications: sacred and profane. If something was judged profane, it was to be destroyed. If it was considered sacred, it was taken over for religious purposes. But consider the obvious difficulties of total destruction in a primitive society and culture. The tearing down of an entire city was no small task. It is not likely that the *herem* was ever really practiced, at least on a very large scale. It was seen more as an ideal that should be accomplished.

In chapter 24, we find the ceremony of the renewal of the covenant made at Mount Sinai. This ceremony was to be held yearly near the city of Shechem, which was located in the valley between two mountains: Mt. Gerizim and Mt. Ebal. In the ceremony, half the tribes would climb Mt. Gerizim and shout the blessings of the covenant across the valley. The other six tribes would climb Mt. Ebal and pronounce the curses that would befall them if the covenant were broken.

In the beginning of chapter 24, we find a long preamble about Yahweh, the God of Israel, which is followed by a history of what he had done for his people. This type of prologue typifies how the Hebrews maintained their history. It was always brought up to the present, thus linking the present with the past. This linking of past and present goes by the technical name *anamnesis.*

After Joshua died, the Hebrews were left leaderless. The next leaders, the Judges, were in charge of small areas, or perhaps, only tribes, and we will see no other leaders of all the people until the time of the kings.

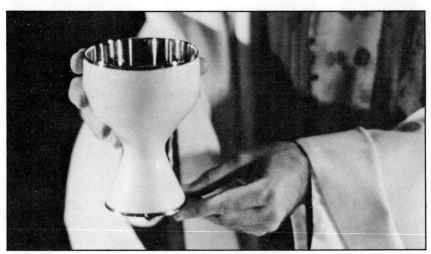

EXERCISES:

1) Every year at the Easter Mass we renew our baptismal promises.
   Is this in any way similar to the covenant renewal ceremony of the Hebrews?

   _____

   _____

   Look up the baptismal promises you made last Easter. What were the conditions of these promises?

   _____

   _____

   _____

2) Look up the term "anamnesis" in a biblical dictionary in the library.
   Explain the meaning of the term in your own words.

   _____

   _____

3) The liturgical celebration of the Mass links the saving action of Jesus with people in the present.
   List the major parts of the Mass.

   _____

   _____

   _____

   How does each part relate to the past? What is it commemorating?

   _____

   _____

   _____

   _____

   _____

JUDGES

Reading: Judges 1, 6-9

Key Idea: The conquest of the Promised Land.

PREVIEW EXERCISE:

Before reading the material from Judges, gather into small groups and discuss the qualities of a folk hero of today.

—Name some folk heroes of our times.

—What are the qualities or achievements that make them stand out?

It is often true that words change their meanings over long periods of time. The title "Judges" is a good example of such a word. In our present-day understanding, a judge is a public official whose job it is to hear and decide court cases. But in the Old Testament, it was a different story.

In this section of the Old Testament, a judge handled legal matters according to the standards of his day. But he was also a military leader—one chosen because of his skill in battle. It was the task of the judges to lead small armies of conquest in the various areas of Palestine.

We must remember that the Book of Joshua gave us an overview of the conquest of the entire area in rather general terms. The Book of Judges is a more localized work, dealing with the particular conquest of a given area. Joshua gave us the impression that the conquest was easy. Judges, however, is more realistic in its description of the invasion by the Hebrews.

In the first chapter, we find statement after statement to the effect that various tribes were quite unsuccessful in their early attempts to gain a foothold in the Promised Land. God had promised to Abraham that he and his people would have a land of their own, but clearly, they would have to fight for it. The reason for the Hebrews' inability to conquer, according to the writer, was their unfaithfulness to Yahweh.

We find the stories of several major and minor judges in this book: Deborah, Ehud, Gideon, Jephtha, and Samson who is perhaps the most famous. For purposes of illustration, we'll examine the story of Gideon. Stories such as those of the judges must have been elaborated upon over the years, as are the stories of any folk hero.

Warfare then, as now, was a rather formidable experience, especially if the enemy had a strong weapon that the other side didn't possess. The enemy—in this case, the Midianites—were raiders from the desert. The camel had been domesticated by now in many parts of the Near East, and the Midianites used them to gain the advantages of speed and mobility over their enemies. The use of camels might not impress the reader as much of a secret weapon. But then, if the other side didn't have them, it was an obvious advantage.

The story begins in chapter 6, where we see the difficulties imposed upon the Hebrews by the Midianites and others who made their lives miserable. Note that the author here used the word "Israelites" rather than "Hebrews"—a rather unusual choice, since the country of Israel didn't exist yet. Obviously, the passage was written long after the events had transpired.

The Midianites and their allies harassed the Hebrews by burning their crops and leaving them no food. The hero, Gideon, was at home harvesting the crops to save them from the Midianite raids. An angel of the Lord appeared to him and said, "Yahweh is with you, valiant warrior!" And, in a rather plaintive reply, Gideon no doubt wondered why, if the Lord *was* with the Israelites, everything was going so poorly. The angel told Gideon of his role in taking on the Midianites. But Gideon objected, insisting that he was not the man for the job. He needed a sign from the Lord that would indicate that he was indeed the one chosen for this mission. This response is a common one in the pages of the Old Testament.

Several stories are intermingled here, but eventually, Gideon became convinced of his new position. To ensure that his upcoming victory over the Midianites was generated by the presence of Yahweh he was allowed to take only 300 soldiers with him into battle. We are not told the number of the opposing force, but the author goes to some length to assure us that the odds were highly in favor of the enemy.

Gideon divided his force into three groups of a hundred men each, and they surrounded the Midianite camp by night. At a pre-arranged signal, they stormed the camp, making lots of noise and confusing the enemy. The Midianites arose from their sleep and, in the confusion, began attacking one another until the force was routed from the territory.

Most of the other stories of the judges are much like this one. It's reasonable to ask why such stories are included in the Old Testament, and what their meaning can be for us.

The stories show, quite simply, that Yahweh was making good his promise to Abraham, Isaac, and Jacob; that they would have a land of their own. They had to fight to obtain it, but eventually they succeeded.

In addition, their success hinged upon their faithfulness to Yahweh. If the people had not been faithful to the covenant, it was unrealistic to expect Yahweh to be with them in battle. If they had been faithful, on the other hand, success would be more likely.

When we study the Old Testament today, we're not really concerned with the historical accuracy of the accounts. Nor are we concerned too much with the accuracy of the details mentioned. Our questions must be more biblically oriented: What did God do for his people? And for the Hebrews in this period of the Old Testament, that was patently obvious.

QUESTIONS:

1) Read the story of Deborah (Jgs 4-5). Mark the scale below indicating your evaluation of her performance as a judge.

Bad   0—1—2—3—4—5—6—7—8—9—10   Good

Discuss why you put the mark where you did. Give reasons based on what you read in the text.

Compare your evaluations with others in the class.

2) Read the story of Samson (Jgs 13-16). Mark the chart below indicating your evaluation of his performance as a judge.

Bad   0—1—2—3—4—5—6—7—8—9—10   Good

Discuss why you put the mark where you did. Give reasons based on what you read in the text.

Compare your evaluations with others in the class.

1 SAMUEL

Reading: 1 Samuel 9-12, 19, 26, 31.

Key Idea: Formation of a national identity.

If we look closely at the above readings, we find that there are two definite strains of thought presented regarding the establishment of a monarchy in Palestine. The pro-monarchial view shows Saul winning a military battle against the Ammonites (chapter 11). He was then made king because of his military prowess and leadership abilities. Less complimentary is the anti-monarchial passage in chapter 10:17-24, in which Saul was merely chosen by lot, and subsequently was found hiding out among the baggage.

The two passages reflect a difficulty that is hard to understand in our own culture. None of us has had the experience of living in a primitive society, or one that has gone from no structure at all to one with a king and all the trappings of royalty. Yet, try to imagine what difficulties faced the young Hebrew nation at this time.

Traditionally, as well as theologically, Israel's king had been Yahweh himself. Various people, such as the judges or Samuel, had spoken for him. In general, this was considered acceptable by the anti-monarchial group. Others believed that a human leader was essential—to lead the nation in war, to beat back the Philistines and other enemies, and to make immediate decisions. Ultimately, the anti-monarchial view lost. It did not admit defeat without stern warnings to the people, though. They would be taxed, since someone had to pay for the new government. The people would be conscripted for war when a fighting force was needed. The king's home would have to be staffed and filled with provisions.

Remember, all of this was being done for the first time. It is reasonable to assume that errors were made as the king worked his way toward an understanding of his role.

Chapter 12 is rather harsh on the new monarchy. In it, Samuel warned the people that they could expect further trouble now that they had a king. He warned them to place Yahweh first and the king second. In fairness, though, Samuel was the one who spoke for Yahweh at that time. It's quite possible that a power struggle had taken place between Saul and Samuel. More accurately, it was a struggle between ideas, and Samuel lost. After all, the people were not about to ignore a successful military leader.

Further reading in the book informs us that Saul led his troops against the Philistines, and drove them from central Palestine. Apparently it was not a crushing defeat, for they reappear with great regularity during Saul's reign. But it was successful in the sense that a large part of Palestine now belonged to the Israelites, and this was one factor in Israel becoming a true nation instead of a tribal confederation.

Undoubtedly, one of the greatest difficulties faced by the new king was the problem of unity. Prior to this time, allegiance had been more tribal than national. With the acquisition of land, and with the necessity of drawing upon all of the tribes for men to supply the army, this attitude began to change. Saul laid the groundwork for later kings to build a nation, largely because of the need for common defense.

Had Saul's reign ended at this point, he would have been remembered more kindly. The stories in this part of the first book of Samuel show that Saul did not always exhibit the best judgment.

It was toward the end of his reign that Saul was confronted by two difficult situations. First, there was continual pressure from the Philistines; second, there was the military success of a young man named David. The pressure was simply more than Saul could handle. You can read of his rather bizarre and eccentric behavior in the section beginning with chapter 19 and continuing throughout the book.

Saul spent so much of his time trying to hunt down and kill David that we can only wonder how the Philistines were kept out of the country. He was unsuccessful in his personal warfare against David, and finally suffered death at the hands of the Philistines in a battle on Mt. Gilboa.

But Saul was successful in many ways. He built up the army, gave the nation the basis for unity, and was victorious in battle. But he was also a tragic figure. He was eccentric at best, and, through his inability to handle the pressures mentioned earlier, was obsessed with the idea of killing David. Surely, his continual personal quest interfered with the daily administrative affairs of the Israelite kingdom.

What lesson can be learned from this episode in Israelite history? Certainly this was an important period, for it represents a new direction for their nation. It also set the stage for the two greatest kings to come: David and Solomon.

Perhaps there is a far more personal lesson than that, especially when we look at the situation with the benefit of hindsight. The people wanted a king, and they got one. But they expected more of him than he was able to provide. It was essential in Israel's history at this time that their new king be a strong religious figure, which Saul wasn't. Leadership was (and still is) moral as well as political or military.

But also, the people were at fault. By emphasizing military victory at the expense of personal leadership, they asked for a wrong value. Saul couldn't provide the religious leadership that the country needed, and Samuel was no longer in a position to do so.

As Saul and his sons lay dying on the battlefield at Mt. Gilboa, it would have been a sobering thought for his people to recall the warning of Samuel at the beginning of Saul's reign:

> Only reverence and serve Yahweh faithfully with all your heart, for you see the great wonder he has done among you. But if you persist in wickedness, you and your king shall perish (1 Sm 12:24-25).

1. List what you believe are all the qualifications of a leader.

2. In your opinion, and based upon your list, was Saul a good leader? Why/why not?

2 SAMUEL

Reading: 2 Samuel 1, 5-7, 11, 12.

Key Idea: Origin of belief in a Messiah.

The story of David actually begins with the struggles he had with Saul. Saul had spent the final years of his reign persecuting David, whom he had thought the most serious threat to his throne.

Feelings between the two men were so bad that, eventually, David was forced to flee. He had gathered around him the nucleus of a small army. It was made up of malcontents, debtors, escaped prisoners, and the like, but it evolved into an effective fighting force. The continuing pressure from Saul and his army finally forced David to flee the country, and he presented himself and his army to the Philistines. At first glance, this might be thought treason, since David was apparently going over to the enemy. For David, though, it was a shrewd political move with no disastrous consequences. While he was with the Philistines, as he would later point out to his critics, he never fought against Israel. And being with the Philistines afforded him protection from Saul.

After Saul was killed on Mt. Gilboa, his son Ishbaal succeeded him as king. At about the same time, David was summoned from the Philistines and made king over the territory of Judah, the southernmost part of Israel. Confrontation with Ishbaal was inevitable.

Chapters 2 through 4 of the Second Book of Samuel describe this tense situation quite graphically, and we are struck by the grim descriptions of personal combat contained here. Ishbaal had neither the skill of David in warfare, nor the loyalty of the people. It was only a matter of time before David won.

When David became king over all Israel, he showed his political skill in three distinct ways. First, he made Jerusalem the civil and religious capital of his kingdom. Jerusalem was centrally located between North and South, and thus was the ideal choice. It was here that the palace and Temple would later be erected.

Second, amid the great celebration described in chapter 6, David brought the Ark of the Covenant into Jerusalem. The Ark, which had been a unifying symbol among the 12 tribes, had lost much of its significance.

The Ark was a moveable chest which contained the Ten Commandments, the staff of Aaron, and a container of manna from the days of wandering in the desert. The first known shrine of the Ark of the Covenant was at Shiloh. The Ark had been captured by the Philistines at one time, but later it was returned. It had been moved from place to place, finally ending up at the town of Kiriath-jearim. It was from there that David brought it to Jerusalem, seeing in the Ark a chance to bring unity to the 12 tribes through a common symbol.

David's third accomplishment was to defeat the Philistines. There had been constant warfare between the Israelites and the Philistines since the earliest days of the Israelite invasion of Canaan, but up through the time of Saul, no one had gained the upper hand. Under David, however, decisive battles were fought, and the Philistines were routed. The Philistines, so strong that they gave their name to the country of Palestine, were never again an effective fighting or cultural force. They simply disappeared from history by intermingling with other cultures.

But David also made several serious errors. Certainly, his sin of adultery with Bathsheba, followed by his murder of her husband Uriah, were tragic and cruel situations. From this point on, the kingship of David began to decline. Toward the end of his reign, several internal revolts took place—one of them led by his own son, Absalom. We must wonder why these revolts were possible, if David were truly as popular as some of the sections of Scripture would have us believe.

From a religious point of view—and that's our real interest—one major event emerged from David's reign. In 2 Samuel 7, we see David's concern for the fact that the Ark of the Covenant resided in a tent. David wanted to build a house for the Ark, and told his plan to his court prophet, Nathan. In response, God told the king through Nathan that he would build a "house" for David—not a building, but a dynasty. We are told that David's "house and kingdom would endure forever."

Ultimately, this belief became known as "messianism." The word *messiah* actually means "anointed one" or "king"; thus, any king could claim the title. The belief became increasingly political and nationalistic over successive generations. So, when Jesus, the true Messiah, actually came, he was largely unrecognized.

The point is that messianism began with David, as did the belief that from David's line would come the Messiah. Later on, when the gospels were written, Matthew and Luke went to great lengths in their respective genealogies to show that Jesus descended from David. Now we can see why: The promise to David was fulfilled in an eternal Messiah who would reign forever. That will, of course, be the story of the New Testament.

DISCUSSION:

David was one of the most important Israelite kings. He was chosen by God for a specific task, and from his descendants would come the Messiah.

Yet, like all other Old Testament figures, David was a human being with strengths and weaknesses, successes and failures.

1. Make a list of David's weaknesses as leader. Why, then, was David considered such a great king?

---

2. Evaluate David's reign on the following scale:

Bad   0—1—2—3—4—5—6—7—8—9—10   Good

Give your reasons for putting the mark where you did. Compare your evaluations with others in the class.

---

1 KINGS—Solomon

Reading: 1 Kings 1, 2, 3, 8, 9.

Key Idea: The growth of the monarchy.

Solomon became king of Israel around the year 960 B.C. Nathan, David's court prophet, had suggested to King David that Solomon be named king when it appeared that others were seeking the throne (chapter 1). Solomon was made king while David was still the official ruler of Israel.

Solomon's initial task, acting upon the advice from his father David, was to make the kingdom secure from revolt by eliminating his enemies. Once Solomon had the kingdom firmly in his grasp, he allied himself with Egypt by marriage to the pharaoh's daughter.

One of Solomon's greatest characteristics was his legendary wisdom. In the third chapter of the book, we find Solomon praying to the Lord for wisdom during his reign, rather than for long life, or riches, or military victory. It is likely that some of Solomon's wisdom is preserved in part, at least, in sections of the Wisdom literature of the Old Testament, particularly in the Book of Proverbs.

The wisdom of Solomon was vast and diverse. Even the queen of Sheba (in Arabia) came to visit him to hear him speak, and also to initiate trade with Israel.

Israel was a relatively wealthy nation during this period but the wealth was not shared among many people. It was in the hands of a few in the ruling class. We find a description of Solomon's wealth in chapter 10:14-29. Here, we are told that:

For riches and for wisdom King Solomon outdid all the kings of the earth. The whole world sought audience of Solomon to hear the wisdom God had implanted in his heart and each would bring his own present: gold vessels, silver vessels, robes, armor, spices, horses and mules; and this went on year after year (1 Kgs 10:23-25).

It is likely that the description is somewhat exaggerated. Nonetheless, it was Israel's greatest period of prosperity.

Another of Solomon's accomplishments was his building of the Temple and the palace. We are told that it took seven years to build the Temple in Jerusalem, and that it was magnificent when completed. This Temple was divided into three areas: the outer porch, the large inner sanctuary, and the cube-shaped Holy of Holies which housed the Ark of the Covenant. When the Temple was completed, it was dedicated to Yahweh. A cloud filled the Temple, and the priests and the people knew that the Lord's glory was present.

Although it took seven years to build the Temple, it took 13 years to build the palace of the king. Such building projects were costly in several ways. First, Solomon used forced labor to undertake such projects. This would later prove to be a serious mistake, because eventually the people would refuse to work under such circumstances. Second, even with Israel's expanded wealth, the country could hardly afford such projects. Solomon had, in effect, given a blank check to the king of Tyre, Hiram I, for his aid in construction. Solomon's additional payment of 20 cities to Hiram seems to indicate that he had overextended both himself and his country.

The wisdom of Solomon seems to have deserted him late in his reign. Solomon had built up a large harem for himself, as a sign of his affluence and power. Even if the numbers in the Bible are inflated, the number was still impressive.

The wives of Solomon's harem were from other countries, and they insisted upon worshiping their own gods. Solomon built temples to these gods and, according to the Scriptures, he even began worshiping them himself.

The decline of the kingdom was swift. Several revolts broke out during this period, and Solomon was unable to maintain effective control. Jeroboam, his own servant, was told by the prophet Ahijah of Shiloh that he would eventually rule over 10 of the 12 tribes. The remainder would go to Solomon's son, Rehoboam. When Solomon discovered the proposed rebellion, he tried to have Jeroboam killed. Jeroboam fled to Egypt, where he remained until Solomon's death in 922 B.C.

Wisdom and power were no guarantees of a successful reign. Solomon had great success in his building programs, but such efforts cost him much popularity when he used forced labor in his construction. And Solomon's wisdom seemed to fail him when he needed it most: in the final years of his reign when he deserted Yahweh and worshiped false gods. The result would be the dissolution of the kingdom after Solomon's death. His kingdom would never regain its former greatness.

Surely, Solomon was aware of all this. He possessed the wisdom necessary to rule fairly, to administer well, to build, to win military victory. The one missing element was his total fidelity to Yahweh. One lesson stands out clearly from this section of the Old Testament: *The knowledge and ability of Solomon in theory was not the same as the knowledge and ability of Solomon on the throne.* Knowledge did not ensure success.

> Yahweh therefore said to Solomon, "Since you behave like this and do not keep my covenant or the laws I laid down for you, I will most surely tear the kingdom away from you and give it to one of your servants. For your father David's sake, however, I will not do this during your lifetime, but will tear it out of your son's hands. . . . For the sake of my servant David, and for the sake of Jerusalem which I have chosen, I will leave your son one tribe" (1 Kgs 11:11-13).

DISCUSSION:

A) In 1 Kings 3:16-28 we read one of the most famous stories of Solomon's wisdom. If necessary, reread the story. Then break up into small groups and discuss the following.

1) What did Solomon do?

2) What special insights into human nature did he show?

3) Think of a story from the New Testament in which Jesus showed great wisdom.

4) Do you know anyone personally who has shown great wisdom?

5) How do you feel about praying for wisdom as Solomon did?

B) Solomon deliberately chose to do wrong. Discuss why he would make such a choice. Do you think there was one big decision involved, or were there a number of smaller decisions made that led up to the final choice? What little decisions do you think he might have made that moved him toward his final decision?

C) Outline the steps that a teenager may have taken on the way to becoming a drug addict or alcoholic. Were some of the early steps morally wrong? Were they wise?

1 KINGS—After Solomon

Reading: 1 Kings 12-14.

Key Idea: Reasons for the division of the kingdom.

It had been difficult for the Israelite kings—even the great ones—to hold the tribal confederation together. The rebellions during the reigns of both David and Solomon, as well as the difficulties created by the forced labor, eventually led to the division of the kingdom.

Solomon died in 922 B.C. He was succeeded by his son, Rehoboam. Rehoboam had a rather strong hold on the southern area of the kingdom since Jerusalem, the capital city, was technically in Judah. But the northern tribes remained rebellious.

Rehoboam went up to the ancient city of Shechem to be proclaimed king. There the people challenged him about continuing the forced-labor policies. Rehoboam's advisors wisely suggested to him that he relent. But he then chose other advisors who suggested that he treat the people even more harshly.

It seems possible from the readings that Rehoboam could have saved the kingdom if he had used the least bit of common sense. But his own arrogance prevailed. The people revolted, and Rehoboam had to flee to the safety of Jerusalem.

Jeroboam, the servant of Solomon, had fled to Egypt after an attempted revolt during Solomon's lifetime. When the northern tribes revolted, rather than submit to Rehoboam, the door was opened for Jeroboam's return. In accord with what had been told him by Ahijah the prophet, he was made king. The northern kingdom under Jeroboam carried the name Israel, and the southern kingdom under Rehoboam was called Judah.

It's rather easy to see the author's point of view in these selections. Essentially the outcome rested on the willingness of the leaders and the people to follow Yahweh. When they were faithful, everything progressed well. When they were unfaithful and sinful, how could they expect Yahweh to be with them?

Jerusalem had been an important city to the united kingdom not only because it was the seat of government, but also because it was the religious center of the country. In opposition, Jeroboam set up religious shrines at Bethel and Dan in the northern kingdom. Obviously he didn't want the people returning to Jerusalem to worship. Such practices might lead to an eventual restoration of the country, and he would no longer be king.

The division of the kingdom was both a political and an economic disaster. During this period, there was both a cold and a hot war between Israel and Judah. Many of Israel's vassal countries gained their independence. The Philistine cities to the south, if not actually free, caused a great deal of trouble for many years. The countries of Ammon and Moab—both in the Transjordan—regained their freedom from Israel. Surely, this had a drastic effect on the economy of the nation. Trade was curtailed, or even made impossible. Tribute from the conquered lands no longer flowed into the treasury.

In chapter 14:25, we find a brief mention of the Egyptian king, Shishak. We are told that in the fifth year of the reign of Rehoboam, Shishak attacked Jerusalem and plundered it. Actually, the raid was far more serious.

Shishak wanted to re-establish an Egyptian influence in Asia, and took advantage of the upheaval in Israel to do so. His own records tell us that he actually captured about 150 cities in Palestine and in the Transjordan during this raid. Then he exacted a heavy tribute which further impoverished Israel and Judah.

The northern kingdom of Israel survived almost exactly 200 years. It was defeated and destroyed by the Assyrians in 721 B.C. The southern kingdom, Judah, lasted until 587 B.C., when it was overrun by the Babylonians. Many of the citizens were deported, and the Exile begun. We will trace these developments later.

These were dark days for the chosen people. It was a period of history in which the leadership went from bad to worse. And, in the mind of the author, the leadership's ability to succeed was directly dependent upon the faithfulness of the king to Yahweh.

We can make a few valid assumptions about this period of history. The author does simplify matters when he claims that a king was a success or a failure, depending upon his personal faithfulness to Yahweh. But it cannot be doubted that religious leadership was lacking. With the new shrines established at Bethel and Dan, it was only a matter of time until the problem of idolatry became a real threat to the religious belief of the people.

Yet, all during this period, it is significant that Yahweh never abandoned his people. The covenant was two-sided, of course. But no matter what happened, it was never God's side of the agreement that had been broken.

FOR DISCUSSION:

The Hebrew term "hesed-Yahweh" is often found in the Old Testament. It refers to God's "covenant-love" for his people. The term refers to God's faithfulness toward the covenant, as well as his mercy to his people when they broke the covenant.

The term also indicates God's love for his people in even initiating the covenant process. There is a continual pattern in all of the Scriptures of God initiating and man responding.

As the monarchy began to draw away from the covenant, God showed his love for his people by always taking them back. Thus, the "hesed-Yahweh" is a key Old Testament idea.

We have a covenant with God today through his son, Jesus. Frequently, through sin, we break that covenant. How does God show his "covenant-love" for us when we break our covenant with him?

2 KINGS

> Reading: 2 Kings 17, 20, 22, 25.
> Key Idea: The defeat of the two kingdoms and the beginning of
> the prophetic movement.

The division of the kingdom of Israel immediately after the death of Solomon was tragic, to say the least. But, as if events weren't bad enough, the period after the division was even worse. To put it simply, the kingship failed badly during this period. In Israel, according to the authors, various evils and the worship of false gods contributed to the downfall of that kingdom. Men such as Omri and Ahab were hardly the religious leaders that the people needed. Such a kingdom could not last.

In 721 B.C., the king of Assyria attacked and defeated the northern kingdom. The Assyrians imprisoned King Hoshea and deported a large percentage of the population. Then they took peoples from other conquered lands and relocated them in the northern kingdom. Such a tactic, obviously, would hinder revolt. It would also change cultural practices and religious beliefs over a long period of time.

The southern kingdom, Judah, fared little better. Generally, the authors of this section judged the monarchy as evil, because the kings were unfaithful to Yahweh, with one or two notable exceptions. A few kings, one of whom was Josiah, did attempt religious reform. Historical circumstances prevented his success, and Josiah was killed in battle in the late 600s B.C.

Judah seemed unwilling to learn from Israel's mistakes. In 597 B.C., Judah was attacked by the Babylonians, the newest power. An unfortunate revolt a few years later sealed Judah's fate. In 587 B.C., the Babylonians again attacked and defeated Jerusalem, apprehended the king, and led off a sizeable percentage of the citizenry into exile.

It seemed as though the covenant was at an end. But throughout this long, tragic period of history, there was one element of hope.

During this time a movement began in Israel known as prophecy. The period of the demise of the kingdoms was also the period of the classical prophets in Israel.

Perhaps no biblical word is more confusing than "prophet." We need only be aware of some of the word's uses today to see the problem. If we want to know what a prophet's role was in Old Testament times, then we'd best look at the Old Testament prophets themselves.

In the next chapter, we will look at some of the more important prophets in ancient Israel. We'll find that their message fits well into this period of Israel's history, and, perhaps, even into our own.

FOR DISCUSSION:

Many of the Hebrews expected their Messiah to be an earthly king—to lead the people in battle, make decisions, and to make Israel great again. Divide the class into discussion groups of no more than five students each, and answer the following questions:

Try to imagine yourself living in ancient Israel. What would be the advantages of having a king? What would you expect that king to do for you and for the country? List all responses. Are any of the responses similar to the Hebrew expectations of the Messiah? Why?

CHAPTER SUMMARY:

1. After the death of Moses, Joshua became the new leader of the Hebrew people and he led them into the Promised Land.

2. The Book of Judges shows the difficulty of conquering Palestine.

3. The success of a leader was directly related to the faithfulness of that leader to Yahweh.

4. Saul was selected as the first king of Israel.

5. God promised King David that from his descendants would come a Messiah.

6. Israel reached its greatest period of wealth under King Solomon.

7. After Solomon's death in 922 B.C., the kingdom was divided.

8. Israel fell to the Assyrians in 721 B.C.

9. Judah fell to the Babylonians in 587 B.C.

CHAPTER THREE IN REVIEW:

1. How does the Old Testament sense of history differ from that of today?

2. If the Book of Judges was more historically accurate than the Book of Joshua, why were both books written covering the same time period?

3. What were the qualifications of an Old Testament judge?

4. How did the books of Joshua and Judges advance the promise that God made to Abraham?

5. Why did so many Israelites oppose the establishment of a monarchy?

6. Evaluate the reign of David. What were his successes and what were his failures?

7. Solomon was king over Israel during the nation's greatest period of prosperity. What caused his downfall?

8. According to the biblical authors, what one characteristic made a king good or bad?

TERMS TO KNOW:

historical books	herem	anti-monarchial view
confederation	anamnesis	
judge	infidelity	Messiah
Transjordan	pro-monarchial view	hesed-Yahweh
		divided kingdom

SPECIAL PROJECT:

Compare the great kings of Israel—Saul, David, and Solomon. Show how each of them advanced the plan that God revealed to Abraham.

4
Prophets and Prophecy

It was during the decline of the kingship that the prophets came forward to give advice to the kings of Israel and to their people. Prophecy in Israel took place from about the seventh through the fifth centuries B.C.

There are 16 prophetic books in the Bible: four major prophets (Isaiah, Jeremiah, Ezekiel, and Daniel) and 12 minor ones. The difference between these two groups is that the major prophets have more recorded detail about themselves and their message than do the minor prophets. But the message of all the prophets was essentially the same.

Some of the prophets lived at the same time as others. Many of them behaved in a rather bizarre fashion when they prophesied, and others did not. But all spoke in their own way for Yahweh. All challenged the people and their leaders to change, and to put the values of their lives back into proper perspective.

Few, if any, of the prophets spent their entire lives in prophecy. Most were called from very ordinary activity and occupations to which they returned when their prophetic task was finished.

If we were to summarize a few of the general characteristics of Old Testament prophecy, they would be as follows:

1. The times in which prophecy occurred were generally good, from the standpoint of material prosperity, for it was then that people seemed to be less aware of God. They didn't need him, so he was forgotten.

2. The prophet used concrete images and specific challenges. Amos, for example, told the women of Samaria to change, or they would be "dragged away with hooks," a reference to the Assyrian mode of deportation.

3. The basic challenge of the prophet was *conversion:* Change your way of life. It was necessary that this conversion take place immediately—later on would be too late. Prophets spoke from a generally *present* orientation.

4. The basic message of the prophet could be phrased: "Repent and be saved." This sums up rather well the key idea of most prophetic books. Of course, the opposite of the statement would be true also: "Fail to change, and you will be lost."

EXERCISE:

A prophet spoke for God when he told the people what God wanted them to do. They were to change their way of life so as to conform to the covenant God had made with them. His message was aggressive and challenging, not usually what the people wanted to hear. As a result the prophet was often rejected.

In contemporary times we hear the term *prophecy* used in relation to telling the future.

1) Is this the same meaning as in Scripture? Why? Why not?

_____

_____

_____

2) Name two contemporary figures who "tell the future," and explain why their prophecy is not the same as biblical prophecy.

_____

_____

_____

_____

3) Name two contemporary figures you believe to be prophets in the biblical sense. Explain why.

_____

_____

_____

There are five parts to most prophetic books. In the first part, God called a person to be a prophet. This could take place through a vision, the appearance of an angel of the Lord, or some recognition of the person involved that God had somehow spoken to him.

The second part of the book listed the charges against the people. The prophet told them specifically how they were violating the covenant. This part of the book was extremely direct, telling the numerous ways that the people had failed.

The third part of the book was the message, in which the prophet actually told the people to change their way of life. No matter what an individual prophet said, his words could usually be condensed into the formula, "Repent and be saved."

The fourth part of the book was the lament of the prophet. He was sorrowful because his people wouldn't listen to him or heed the word of the Lord. Usually, he genuinely wished for the conversion of his people, and had no desire to see them suffer.

The final part of the book was the rejection of the prophet and his message by the people. A prophet was almost always doomed to failure, because most people were comfortable living life the way they always had. They didn't want someone going around telling them that they had to change.

EXERCISE:

Complete the following statements:

1. These are the situations in my school that I think a present-day prophet would speak about:

---

2. These are the situations in society that I think a present-day prophet would speak about:

ISAIAH

Reading: Isaiah 1, 2, 6, 7, 50, 53.

Key Idea: A call to conversion.

In the southern kingdom during the seventh and sixth centuries B.C., there came a true crisis of faith. Religious beliefs and practices had dwindled to a sorry state. The moral fiber of Judah had broken down; there was a tremendous gap between what the people of God were supposed to be and what they had become.

Into this situation came the prophet Isaiah, one of the most important prophets of the entire Old Testament. Isaiah's task was to win the people back to Yahweh: to challenge their way of life, to correct their priorities. He was the conscience of the nation during this period, and his writings serve as an accurate indicator of its problems.

As we take a brief look at the Book of Isaiah, we should realize that it was actually written in three distinct periods of time. The first part of the book, chapters 1-39, contains poems and oracles from the time of Isaiah or that of his immediate disciples. This is the section of the book that challenges the people to change. The second part of the book, chapters 40-55, is called Deutero-Isaiah and may have been written as long as 200 years later. It describes the coming Messiah as a suffering servant. The final chapters (56-66) are called Trito-Isaiah, and tell of the coming of the kingdom of Yahweh and may have been written before the exile to Babylon. Our main concern is with the first section of the book, and with the statements of the prophet himself.

One of the major sections of any prophetic book is the part that tells us exactly what the people were doing wrong. This "indictment" of the people begins in chapter 1 of Isaiah. The people had forgotten the Lord, and had sinned against him. Their sacrifices were worthless because they were insincere. The people were told that they had to practice justice, listen to the pleas of the orphan and the widow, and show sincerity in all they did.

To best understand the flavor of Isaiah's prophecy, read chapters 1 and 2 aloud, trying to emphasize the forcefulness of the passages. Such a technique would convince you very quickly that Isaiah was issuing a genuine challenge to his people.

Prophets "called the people to conversion," and this is a phrase we must understand well. When the word "conversion" is used, we often think of changing religions. That's not what the prophets meant, however. They meant, rather, the idea of people turning their whole life around; of turning back to God. The people were to hear the prophet's words, examine their lives in the light of them, and then turn *away* from their sin and their misdeeds, and turn back toward Yahweh. Conversion was not a one-time situation, such as changing religions might be. Rather, it was a gradual lifetime process.

In chapter 6, we find the actual call of Isaiah as a prophet. This is rather curious, since he had already been prophesying for five chapters. We must recognize, however, that the text of Isaiah has suffered much over the years, and is not in perfect order. Again, however, *it is the religious message that is most important.* In this chapter, Isaiah was called by God through a remarkable vision.

Chapter 7 contains one of Isaiah's messianic prophecies. The king of Judah, Ahaz, was looking for a sign from God to show him that God was still on his side in an upcoming battle. Isaiah responded:

> The Lord himself, therefore,
> will give you a sign.
> It is this: the maiden is with child
> and will soon give birth to a son
> whom she will call Immanuel. . . .
> For before this child knows how to refuse evil
> and choose good,
> the land whose two kings terrify you
> will be deserted (Is 7:14-16).

We have seen that the word *messiah* means "anointed one," or even "king." It could rightly be used by many people. Some of the

Hebrews were looking for the coming of another great king like David. Isaiah's response to Ahaz was rather direct: He would have his sign. A woman would bear a child under rather specific circumstances; when this occurred, Ahaz need fear his enemies no longer.

Christians have always considered this sign to be fulfilled ultimately in Jesus Christ (*christos* is the Greek translation for *messiah*). But it is a sign that operates on two different levels. What the passage means to us today might not have been what it meant in the lifetime of Ahaz and Isaiah. Yes, the passage refers to Jesus, the coming Messiah. But what exactly did it mean to Ahaz, some 700 years earlier? Surely, if the coming of Jesus is the only meaning, it wasn't a very effective sign for King Ahaz, who would never have lived to see it. It wouldn't answer his immediate problem.

Most scholars hold that it's possible for a prophet to speak words to people in his own time that have a fuller meaning than the prophet realized when he spoke them. One does not have to be fully conscious of the workings of God for God's workings to occur. Isaiah, in speaking to his own people in his own time, said something that God wanted said also to people in a later time, or even perhaps to all people of all time. We have to leave room for God to act in the Scriptures.

The second section of the book, Deutero-Isaiah, contains the passages known as the Suffering Servant Songs. There are four of them, and two were included in our readings.

Again, many people had been hoping for a Messiah that would be a great king like David. But the disciples of Isaiah during the Exile (the group called Deutero-Isaiah) changed this understanding in two ways. First, the coming Messiah would be a servant—one who spent his life for others. Also, in a radical change in the idea of messiahship, the Messiah would have to suffer.

As the concept of messiah developed and became somewhat nationalistic, it's easy to understand why Deutero-Isaiah's ideas were rejected. They didn't fit the popular awareness of what the Messiah should be. They were rejected, that is, until the early part of the first century A.D. when the Messiah actually came. When he did come, he assumed both the role of service to others and the role of suffering. The Messiah was Jesus of Nazareth.

EXERCISE:

Read the following passages in Isaiah:

Isaiah 9:5-6

Isaiah 11:1-9

These are frequently called "messianic" passages. The church has always seen their ultimate fulfillment in Jesus Christ. "Messiah," however, indicated that these descriptions could be applied to any future Israelite king. The very word *messiah* means "anointed one," and the kings were the anointed leaders of the people of Israel. These passages have a general fulfillment in the time of the prophet, but they have a unique fulfillment in Jesus Christ.

1) Make a list of the messianic titles found in these two passages from Isaiah.

_____

_____

What kind of a king do you think these passages indicate the Messiah would be? Does your description fit what the Jewish nation was expecting at the time of Christ? Explain.

_____

_____

_____

2) In your own words describe the reign of the Messiah as envisioned by Isaiah.

_____

_____

_____

_____

JEREMIAH

Reading: Jeremiah 1, 5, 12, 16, 19, 31.

Key Idea: A return to the covenant with Yahweh.

Jeremiah was called to be a prophet in the latter part of the sixth century B.C. He prophesied to the people of the southern kingdom of Judah. We can read of his call in the first chapter of the book. Evidently, Jeremiah was rather young when he received the prophetic call (1:5).

Jeremiah wanted to call his people's attention to their own unfaithfulness to Yahweh. He did so by using the rather graphic example of adultery. When two people marry, they commit themselves to each other, to the exclusion of all other persons. Thus, adultery is not only a sexual sin, but perhaps far more seriously, a sin against justice. It was not without reason that Jeremiah chose this image for Judah. For, just like the adulteress, Judah had turned away from her commitment to Yahweh. She did not learn a lesson from what had happened to the northern kingdom of Israel, which had been destroyed by the Assyrians in 721 B.C.

This prophet spoke out rather strongly. In chapter 5, the reader is asked to

> Rove to and fro through the streets of Jerusalem,
> look, now, and learn,
> search her squares;
> if you can find a man,
> one man who does right
> and seeks the truth,
> then I will pardon her,
> says Yahweh (Jer 5:1).

Jeremiah simply didn't believe that Judah could actually turn her back on the God who had done so much for the nation. We find chapter after chapter of Jeremiah's warnings to the people to return to the Lord.

Being a prophet was no easy task. The prophet had the good of the people at heart—he wanted them to return to the Lord and change their lives. Generally speaking, however, people are rather comfortable in the morality they choose, or they wouldn't choose to remain in it. Thus the prophet was destined to an unhappy career. At first, the people would tolerate him. But the tolerance would turn to hostility, and even outright contempt, as they urged the prophet to leave them alone.

We see how this must have affected Jeremiah when we read chapter 12. This chapter is essentially a conversation between Jeremiah and God. Jeremiah had suffered the taunts of his people, and had begun to debate the wisdom of his being chosen for the prophetic ministry.

If life had become difficult for Jeremiah rather early, it only became worse later on. In chapter 16, we see that Jeremiah's very life was to be a symbol to the people, since they refused to accept his words. He was not allowed to marry; he could not offer sympathy to the families of those who had died. He could not celebrate publicly. Why couldn't he?

> When you tell this people all these words and they ask you, "Why has Yahweh decreed this appalling disaster for us? What is our crime? What sin have we committed against Yahweh our God?" then you are to answer, "It is because your ancestors abandoned me—it is Yahweh who speaks—and followed alien gods, and served and worshipped them. . . . And you for your part have behaved even worse than your ancestors" (Jer 16:10-12).

Thus his prophecy was not only spoken; it was also acted out. This type of prophecy is called "symbolic prophecy." A good example is found in chapter 19, when Jeremiah gathered some of the notables of the city out by the local trash dump. He brought with him a large clay pot. In the presence of the people gathered there, he took the large earthenware pot, raised it dramatically over his head, and hurled it down to the ground where it shattered into fragments.

When the people asked why he did this, his response was clear and frightening:

> Yahweh Sabaoth says this: "I am going to break this people and this city just as one breaks a potter's pot, irreparably" (Jer 19:11).

Historical events proved Jeremiah correct. The people didn't change, and finally the kingdom of Judah was besieged by the Babylonians. Jerusalem fell in July of 587 B.C., and many of the leading citizens were exiled into Babylon. Had we been in Jeremiah's position, our probable response would have been, "I told you so." Fortunately for Judah, Jeremiah was a much greater man than that, and would offer them hope.

To understand his true importance, we have to be aware of a few historical circumstances. The Sinai Covenant, from the time of Moses, had been one of the pillars of Israelite theology. It was best expressed in the covenantal formula: "If you obey my statutes and laws, I will be your God and you will be my people." This belief sustained and nourished the people throughout some of the more difficult periods of their history.

The Davidic Covenant—the covenant that God had made with David—was another such pillar. It came from a later period of history than the Sinai Covenant, and reflected the belief that from David's line would come the long-awaited Messiah.

David had reigned in Jerusalem—the southern kingdom—so the Davidic Covenant had far more importance there than it did in Israel in the north. In their great emphasis on Jerusalem as the city of David, on the presence of Yahweh at the Temple in Jerusalem, and even upon their own expectations, the Jews simply couldn't believe that God would ever let Jerusalem fall. This led to a complacency that tended to overlook the Sinai Covenant.

Even though Jeremiah was raised in the southern kingdom of Judah (the town of Anathoth), he knew well the Sinai Covenant of

the northern kingdom. When the great tragedy of the collapse and fall of Jerusalem came, and the people thought that Yahweh had let them down, Jeremiah was able to offer hope and consolation.

In chapter 31:31, we find his "new covenant." In fact, it sounds suspiciously like the Sinai Covenant of old. But it *was* new to the people who were hearing it—the exiles of the kingdom of Judah. Jeremiah reminded them of the necessity of being faithful to Yahweh, and then the covenant would be kept. He gave his people hope during a period of national despair.

It's easy for us today to sit back and wonder how the Israelites could have been so unfaithful to Yahweh, especially after all he had done for them over the years. But we have an even greater covenant—a covenant with God through the blood of his Son Jesus. And by our own lives and actions we repeatedly choose to do wrong, to sin, to fail.

Maybe Jeremiah, and others like him, can be reminders to each of us that we are continually called to grow by turning away from sin, and by turning back to God.

QUESTIONS:

1) The false prophet did not speak for God. He would try to tell the people that the future was bright, when what they really needed was the challenge of the true prophet to change their very lives. Read Jeremiah 23:16-28 for a description of the false prophet. Make a listing of the characteristics of the false prophet. Why do you suppose such people were popular?

---

2) Read Jeremiah 1:4-10. Jeremiah was a young man when he was called by the Lord to be a prophet. He claimed that he was too young to speak for the Lord. What did the Lord tell him?

How old do you think a person has to be for prophetic ministry? Why?

_____

_____

Jeremiah was unpopular because he stood up for what he believed in. He preached what he knew the Lord wanted of his people and frequently went against the crowd by proclaiming what was right rather than what was popular.

Break up into groups of five or six students and discuss the following:

1) If we know the difference between right and wrong, why do we sometimes choose that which is wrong?

2) How much does the crowd influence what we think or do?

FOR PERSONAL REFLECTION:

Rate the influence of the crowd on you in these situations:

1) On the clothes you wear. Look at how your classmates are dressed. How much does this influence what you wear?

   None   0—1—2—3—4—5—6—7—8—9—10   A lot

2) On your hair style. Look at the hair styles of people your age. How much does this influence how you wear your hair?

   None   0—1—2—3—4—5—6—7—8—9—10   A lot

3) On your activities. How do most of your friends spend their free time? Are they involved in sports, school-related activities, part-time jobs, watching TV, cruising? How do you spend your free time? How much do your friends' activities influence what you do?

   None   0—1—2—3—4—5—6—7—8—9—10   A lot

4) Your attitude toward religion. What is the attitude of your friends and classmates toward their faith? How much does this influence what you do?

   None   0—1—2—3—4—5—6—7—8—9—10   A lot

AMOS

Reading: Amos 3, 4, 5, 9.

Key Idea: Change your life for the better.

Amos, a minor prophet from Tekoa in Judah, received the prophetic calling in the mid-seventh century B.C. Although he lived in the southern kingdom, he preached his prophetic message to the people of Israel in the north. He was a shepherd, and possibly returned to that occupation later in his life after his prophetic ministry had ended.

The first two chapters of the book were intended primarily as an attention-getting device. Amos first drew a crowd to listen to him. He did so by speaking out about something other than his intended message. He preached against several countries that were traditional enemies of the Israelites. When a crowd gathered—most likely in total agreement with what he was saying—he then turned to his prophetic message.

If we wanted to do the same thing today, we would drag our soapbox over to the local neighborhood park, climb up, and begin speaking out about some generally accepted evil. Then, when we had a sufficient crowd in general agreement with us, we'd start talking about what was *really* on our minds.

In the third chapter of the book, Amos asked a series of rhetorical questions (a question to which there is no expected reply). The implication was, "If a prophet of the Lord is going to speak, shouldn't you listen?"

The prophet then began to list his charges against the people. Apparently, there were two groups in Israel at this time: a small, extremely wealthy group, and the much larger poor group. Amos preached a message that was a strong challenge to the people of the northern kingdom. He told them:

> Listen to the word, you cows of Bashan
> living in the mountain of Samaria,
> oppressing the needy, crushing the poor,
> saying to your husbands, "Bring us something to drink!"
> The Lord Yahweh swears this by his holiness:
> The days are coming to you now
> when you will be dragged out with hooks . . . (Am 4: 1-2).

We find a new idea emerging in chapter 5: the Day of the Lord. The Israelites had hoped for this day, when Yahweh would vindicate Israel and destroy all her enemies. But Amos changed the concept radically. On that day, Israel would also be punished. It would be a day of "darkness, not light" (5:18 ff).

Worship in the time of Amos was in a sorry state. It had become empty ritual without meaning because it wasn't practiced in the daily lives of the people. Amos challenged the Israelite nation—and us—when he spoke for Yahweh:

> I hate and despise your feasts,
> I take no pleasure in your solemn festivals . . .
> I reject your oblations,
> and refuse to look at your sacrifices of fattened cattle. . . .
> But let justice flow like water,
> and integrity like an unfailing stream (Am 5:21-24).

The king of Israel, Jeroboam, heard of the preaching of Amos through Amaziah, the priest of Bethel. Amaziah complained about the harsh message, and he tried to drive Amos away, calling into question Amos's prophetic credentials. Amos responded by justifying himself, and then prophesying against Amaziah personally (see 7:17).

The book seems rather harsh in its condemnation of the practices of Israel, and it's a bit surprising to see this emphasis change in the midst of chapter 9 (in verse 8, to be exact). For exactly this reason, many commentators believe that verses 8 through 15 are a later addition to the book.

Just after saying that God would destroy Israel completely from the face of the earth (9:8a), he then says that he will *not* destroy it *completely* (9:8b). Amos, or perhaps a later author, realized that there would always be a small group of people doing what they were supposed to be doing. They would be the ones spared from the general destruction to come. The prophets called this group "the remnant," and some of the New Testament writers used this term to describe the church.

When Amos spoke out during a period of Israel's prosperity, he challenged the people to look at their priorities. Many were too secure in the fact that they descended from Abraham, and rejected the message of Amos, although later historical events proved him correct.

Perhaps there is a message for us too. We have to evaluate our own lives from time to time to see where we're going. Amos challenges us as well as his own people. Are we too complacent or comfortable? Are we aware of the abuses or injustices that go on around us? Are we too secure and smug in our Christianity to grow more deeply in our faith? Is worship more than a Sunday ritual for us? Amos calls us to accountability on such questions, and thus he continues to challenge people with his message even today.

DISCUSSION:

Break up into groups of five or six students each and discuss the following statements.

1) God cares how I live my life.
2) Old Testament prophets have little to say to us today.
3) My main responsibility is to myself. I don't have to worry about others.
4) Whatever I do is OK as long as I don't bother other people.

HOSEA

Reading: Hosea 1, 2, 4, 11, 14.

Key Idea: Hosea's life as a symbol for Yahweh's love.

Symbolic prophecy, as we saw in the section on Jeremiah, is prophecy that was acted out. A prophet may spend some small portion of his ministry showing people by his own actions what would happen to them if they did not change.

Occasionally, however, we are confronted by a prophet whose whole adult life was a symbol. Such a man was the prophet Hosea, a prophet of the seventh century B.C. He preached to Israel, and possibly even saw its destruction.

The Book of Hosea deals first with symbolic prophecy by relating the story of his tragic marriage to an unfaithful wife. Then the book deals with the crimes of Israel and its punishment.

In the first section of the book, Hosea was told to go out and marry a prostitute, because the country itself had become nothing but a prostitute through its unfaithfulness to Yahweh. Hosea married a harlot named Gomer, and initially at least, their relationship was fairly stable. She bore Hosea two sons and a daughter.

But Gomer was unable to forget her past, and she went out seeking other lovers with their gifts. She failed to recognize that all of her sustenance came from Hosea himself.

Hosea was torn between his love for his wife Gomer and her rejection. But Hosea's love for Gomer prevailed. He bought her back, redeeming her from her lovers, and restored her to her former position as wife. Even though he had been badly hurt by her actions, his love for her was sufficient to overcome the monumental problems they faced together.

Often, as mentioned earlier, adultery was used by the prophets as a symbol for unfaithfulness to God. Hosea used his own marriage to Gomer to portray the tragedy between Yahweh and Israel. Hosea had been faithful to Gomer, but she had rejected him and chased after others. Ultimately his love would win her back.

It was the same between Yahweh and Israel. Israel was the spouse of Yahweh. He had been faithful to her, supplied her needs, and even gave her a land of her own. But she had rejected him, giving herself to other gods. Like Hosea, he would chastise her in order that, eventually, his love would bring her back to him.

We find Hosea's listing of Israel's crimes in chapter 4:

> Sons of Israel, listen to the word of Yahweh,
> for Yahweh indicts the inhabitants of the country:
> there is no fidelity, no tenderness,
> no knowledge of God in the country,
> only perjury and lies, slaughter, theft,
> adultery and violence, murder after murder (Hos 4:1-2).

Hosea also complained that the priests, who were to be the spiritual leaders of the people, were no better than the people they led. They were the ones who turned the people away from God's law.

Even the monarchy failed to escape the prophet's wrath. In chapter 7:3-7, Hosea charged the king with failure to follow Yahweh. Obviously, to challenge the personal lifestyle of the king was a dangerous action.

Like nearly all true prophets, Hosea and his message were both rejected. The people said that he was a fool, or even mad. Hosea's response was probably rather accurate:

> Ah, yes, but only because your iniquity is so great,
> your apostasy so grave (Hos 9:7).

Chapter 11 of Hosea is a beautiful theological expression of God's love for his people. It also shows, in a poetic way, the suffering of Yahweh when rejected by his people.

The book of Hosea ends on a hopeful note. The possibility of Israel's return to God was left open, although historically this didn't happen. Israel was destroyed by the Assyrians in 721 B.C.

It's quite possible that the inhabitants of the southern kingdom of Judah read the words of Hosea, but they too failed to heed the message. Hosea showed Israel and Judah that God's love was constant and eternal. They were the ones who separated themselves from it by their own selfishness.

EXERCISE:

The relationship between Hosea and his wife Gomer paralleled the relationship between Yahweh and Israel. Gomer had been unfaithful, but Hosea's love had won her back. Yahweh hoped to do the same with his unfaithful people.

Circle one number in each of the following statements, indicating what you believe. Be prepared to discuss your opinions with others in your class.

1. Love is the attraction of one person for another.

   Disagree   1—2—3—4—5—6—7—8—9—10   Agree

2. Love means that you're more concerned about the other person than you are about yourself.

   Disagree   1—2—3—4—5—6—7—8—9—10   Agree

3. Love means that "you never have to say you're sorry."

   Disagree   1—2—3—4—5—6—7—8—9—10   Agree

4. Love means discipline, correcting the other person when he or she does wrong.

   Disagree   1—2—3—4—5—6—7—8—9—10   Agree

5. Love means trust, believing in the other person.

   Disagree   1—2—3—4—5—6—7—8—9—10   Agree

6. Love means consistency, that nothing can change the relationship between two people.

   Disagree   1—2—3—4—5—6—7—8—9—10   Agree

7. Love means fidelity—no involvement with anyone else.

   Disagree   1—2—3—4—5—6—7—8—9—10   Agree

8. Love means forgiveness, even though the other person has hurt you deeply.

   Disagree   1—2—3—4—5—6—7—8—9—10   Agree

MICAH

Reading: Micah 2, 4, 6, 7.

Key Idea: The judgment of the Lord.

Micah was a minor prophet who came from Moresheth, a small town located near the border between Israel and Judah. He preached against both Samaria and Jerusalem; thus he preached against both kingdoms, since these were their two capital cities. But it's likely that his message was heard or read more in the south than in the north, since by that time Israel was quite close to collapse.

The first three chapters of the book remind us of the preaching of two other minor prophets—Amos and Hosea. Micah began in the same way, by listing the sins of the people. Since no one appreciates being told that he or she is doing wrong, we can imagine the general reaction when Micah began to challenge the people.

> Seizing the fields that they covet,
> they take over houses as well,
> owner and house they confiscate together . . . (Mi 2:2).

Prophets, it seems, always look on the bleak side of life. Most of the people who hear them seem to try to avoid the challenge. So it was with Micah—his people were uninterested.

> "Do not rave," they rave
> "do not rave like this.
> No shame is going to overtake us.
> Can the House of Jacob be accursed?
> Has Yahweh lost patience?
> Is that his way of going to work?
> Surely his words are words of kindness
> for his people Israel?" (Mi 2:6-7).

The response of the people to Micah was quite predictable, and quite like the contemporary dictum: "No problem is so big and complex in this life that it can't be ignored." The people couldn't believe that their country would fall, or that they were in any personal danger.

In chapter 3, we find a highly descriptive version of what would happen to the leaders who had led the people astray. They were hardly leaders, but rather obviously people who were interested only in themselves.

Chapter 4 tells of a great future when the nation would be restored. Micah was unclear about when this was to occur. It would be at some vague future date, perhaps at the end of the Exile. The passage contains a beautiful poetic description of life in Jerusalem when Yahweh would again be living in the midst of his people. It describes the peace and blessings that would come to God's chosen people.

A curious passage occurs in this chapter. Chapter 4:1-3 of Micah has the same wording as chapter 2:2-4 of Isaiah. It's true that Isaiah and Micah were contemporaries. Whether or not they ever heard one another preach, though, is not known. Most commentators believe that it was Isaiah who was responsible for the passage, rather than Micah, although there's no way to prove this position. But Micah's copying of the statement would indicate at least a familiarity with the Isaian material.

In chapter 5, we find once again the concept of "remnant," those people earnestly seeking to do the will of the Lord. According to Micah, these people would be the ones to lead their nation back to Yahweh.

Chapter 6 reverts to an earlier situation in the book. It lists again the sins and crimes of the nation. An impressive passage tells us what the people *should* have been doing:

> What is good has been explained to you, man;
> this is what Yahweh asks of you:
> only this, to act justly,
> to love tenderly
> and walk humbly with your God (Mi 6:8).

Yet, this had *not* been happening. Micah claimed that the people were filled with greed and violence. Even worse, they had "kept the laws of Omri and followed all the practices of the House of Ahab" (Mi 6:16), two kings of Israel notorious for their social injustice and their worship of false gods.

The last chapter of the book reminds us somewhat of the writings of Amos. It begins by telling us how Micah challenged the people, saying that they would suffer God's judgment. Then, the mood shifts to a rather hopeful and optimistic note about future restoration. Just as in Amos, many biblical commentators believe that this part of the chapter was a later addition to the book, written perhaps when the people were in exile in Babylon.

The people, especially when in the midst of the exile, would eventually come to the realization that they had done wrong. They would turn to the prophetic writings for hope and encouragement, since the prophets had been correct about other matters that had transpired.

In many ways, the era of the prophets parallels our own era, for many of the same evils still exist. The prophets tried to awaken the slumbering consciousness of their nation; much of what they said applies to us as well. Much of the challenge of the prophets doesn't really interest us today—any more than it interested Judah or Israel—because we simply don't want to hear it. But many of the evils the prophets spoke against still remain in our culture, and even in our individual lives. We must be aware of the message of these prophetic individuals, since they challenged their own people long ago, and continue to challenge us through their written word today.

Micah said that mankind had been told what to do: Act justly, love tenderly, and walk humbly with God. For those of us who call ourselves Christian, that's a good understanding of what it means to live out the gospel.

EXERCISE:

1. What were some of the evils that Micah preached about in his prophetic ministry?

2. Are any of these same situations found in some way today? Which ones?

3. Could Micah be called a "contemporary" prophet? Why/why not?

4. Micah is known as one of the minor prophets. What does this mean, and how does it affect his message?

FOR CLASS DISCUSSION:

Break up into groups of five or six students each. What would a prophet today have to say about the following issues?

corruption in government   abortion

nuclear disarmament   political refugees

women's rights   the welfare system

energy conservation

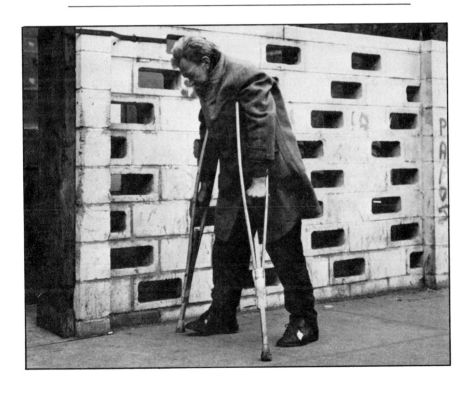

EZEKIEL

Reading: Ezekiel 1, 4, 5, 10, 12, 33, 37.

Key Idea: Preparing the people for the fall of Jerusalem.

During the period surrounding the exile, there were many great prophets in Judah. Most of them preached to the citizens of Jerusalem, urging them to change their ways or suffer the consequences. The fall of Judah, with the exile of its citizens to Babylon, eventually occurred anyway in 587 B.C.

Ten years earlier, Jerusalem had been attacked by the Babylonians. Most of Jerusalem's religious leaders and some of the prominent citizens had been deported, and were in Babylon when the actual fall of Jerusalem occurred.

One of the leaders sent to Babylon was Ezekiel. There he received his calling to the prophetic ministry. His mission was to preach to his people already in exile, rather than to the people in Jerusalem. He was to warn the exiles that the *unthinkable* would happen—that Jerusalem would fall, and that they would be joined in exile by a larger group of the citizenry.

In the first chapter we can find Ezekiel's description of his incredible vision of Yahweh. Such descriptions are often misinterpreted unless we understand some of the Old Testament modes of writing. Some modern-day readers of Ezekiel claim that he had perhaps taken some sort of hallucinogen, or even that he had seen a UFO. Such views simply aren't faithful to the Scriptures. Besides, there seems to be no doubt whatsoever in Ezekiel's mind as to what he had seen.

It was something that looked like the glory of Yahweh (Ez 1:28).

After the vision, Ezekiel was struck dumb, unable to speak. Only when God spoke through him would he be able to say anything at all.

In much of the book, Ezekiel's behavior appears to have been rather eccentric. But we should remember that much of Ezekiel's prophecy is *symbolic* prophecy—prophecy that is acted out. He was trying to convey a message to the people by what he did rather than by what he said.

One of Ezekiel's strongest prophetic actions is found in chapter 5. He built a miniature city, and then hurled verbal threats against it. Then he cut off all the hair of his head and beard, and divided it into three parts. He burned the first portion within the confines of the miniature city. The second part he placed around the small city, and chopped at it with the sword. The final third he threw into the wind; then he scattered it and pursued it with the sword. The hair represented the inhabitants of Jerusalem, and Ezekiel's actions showed what would happen to them in the days to come.

In chapter 10, Ezekiel saw his vision of Yahweh's glory again. It was the same as the vision in chapter 1, except that in this case, the vision was rising up from the Temple and going away from the city. To Ezekiel, the meaning was obvious: Yahweh could no longer tolerate the wickedness of the inhabitants of Jerusalem, and he was abandoning the city to the Babylonians. It wasn't so much that God was rejecting his people; rather, they were driving him away.

The symbolism of chapter 12 is explained in the text itself. Ezekiel showed by his actions what would happen to the leaders of his people—they would be captured by the Babylonians and led away into exile.

The whole mood of the book changes in chapter 33. Ezekiel had been prophesying to the first group of exiles for several years, and most of them would not take him seriously. Because of the promise God had made to David, they believed that God would never allow Jerusalem to fall. Chapter 33 tells us:

> In the twelfth year of our captivity, on the fifth day of the tenth month, a fugitive arrived from Jerusalem and said to me, "the city has been taken." Now the hand of

the Lord had come upon me . . . he had opened my
mouth . . . and I was dumb no longer (Ez 33:21-22).

Ezekiel was vindicated before his countrymen. Perhaps at this
point, he could have ended his prophetic career, taking some comfort
in the idea that his warnings had been fulfilled.

But Yahweh had other plans for him. As the newly exiled people
joined Ezekiel in Babylon, the prophet became aware that it was now
his responsibility to give his people hope and encouragement.

In chapter 37 we find one of the many hopeful signs for the
future. Ezekiel had another vision. He stood in the midst of a field of
dry bones. As he prophesied over them, bones joined together, and
were covered with flesh and skin. Then spirit came into them, and
they came to life. The purpose of this vision was to symbolize the
restoration of the people: The Lord would raise them up and bring
them back to the land of Israel, and they would know that he was the
Lord.

The book concludes with several chapters of hopeful imagery.
The people were told of the building of the New Temple, the New
Jerusalem, and the Lord's triumphant return to his people—all sym-
bols of a bright and hopeful future.

We've only looked at a few of the prophets; a sampling of this
type of biblical literature. There is a certain sameness to what all the
prophets say and do. But that's only because there is such a terrible
sameness about man's sin and selfishness that the prophets had to
oppose. That's why their message is still valid for us today.

Much more could be said about the prophets, or we could look
at some of the other prophetic books. But by now, we can see their
purpose in the history of salvation: to call the people to conversion—to a return to Yahweh in their lives.

EXERCISE:

Once Jerusalem fell to the Babylonians and Ezekiel was vindicated before his countrymen, he could have ended his mission. But he did not. He recognized that he had a new mission—that is, to offer hope to his people in a time of national despair.

He used a type of literature known as "apocalyptic" to do this. Apocalyptic literature was an outgrowth of the prophetic movement.

Unlike prophecy, it generally occurred when times were bad. At this point in Israelite history, there was national despair because of the exile. The apocalyptic writer used signs, visions, dreams, symbols, and numbers to get across his message, unlike the specific descriptions of the prophet. The apocalyptic message was one of hope: Ultimately good would triumph over evil.

Read the following passage:

Ezekiel 40-48

This section of Ezekiel gave the people hope that God would deliver them from the exile and restore them to their homeland.

1. Why did Ezekiel change from prophetic to apocalyptic writing?

_____

_____

_____

_____

2. What is the meaning of the vision of the "heavenly Jerusalem" in chapters 40-48?

_____

_____

_____

_____

3. Ezekiel's eccentric behavior may have been an attempt to gain a wider audience for his prophetic message. Can you find any current examples in the news where other people have acted in an unusual fashion to dramatize their message?

CHAPTER SUMMARY:

1. Basically, a prophet challenged the people to change their way of life.

2. The true prophet spoke for Yahweh.

3. The Book of Isaiah came from three distinct periods of time.

4. The author of the second part of the Book of Isaiah expected that the Messiah would be a suffering servant.

5. *Messiah* means "anointed one."

6. Prophets spoke to people in their own lifetime, but also for people who would come later.

7. Jeremiah preached the Sinai Covenant to people who were familiar only with the Davidic Covenant.

8. Prophecy that is acted out is called "symbolic prophecy."

9. The relationship between Hosea and his wife paralleled the relationship between Yahweh and his people.

10. Ezekiel preached to people who were already in exile.

11. After Judah fell, Ezekiel began preaching a message of hope, rather than a message of despair.

12. Apocalyptic literature is an outgrowth of prophecy.

CHAPTER FOUR IN REVIEW:

1. What is prophecy? What are the major characteristics of prophecy?

2. What is the difference between a major prophet and a minor prophet?

3. What does it mean when a prophet "calls his people to conversion"?

4. Why was Jeremiah's "new covenant" not really new at all?

5. Why did the prophets often use the symbol of adultery for idolatry?

6. Are there people today who are faithful to the basic ideas of Old Testament prophecy? Could they be called prophets?

TERMS TO KNOW:

prophet	Deutero-Isaiah	Trito-Isaiah
Messiah	messianic prophecy	christos
suffering servant	symbolic prophecy	exile
Sinai Covenant	Davidic Covenant	remnant
lament	apocalyptic	false prophet
conversion	major prophet	

SPECIAL PROJECT:

Interview five different people outside your class. Ask them to identify present-day people whom they believe to be prophets. Ask them why they chose these people. Compare your interviews with others in your class.

5
The Wisdom Literature

Much of the material of the Old Testament can be categorized rather easily. The Pentateuch, for example, dealt with the primitive law of Israel. Other books were historical in character. Another specific group of books was prophetic in its outlook. But one group of Old Testament writings seems to defy such a distinct classification, and that group is known collectively as the wisdom literature.

Many ancient countries had wisdom collections. They were generally written by professional scribes, and were often used for the education and instruction of young people.

The basic purpose of wisdom literature was to pass down the prevailing wisdom of one age to another; to pass on what is called "common sense" wisdom. Through wisdom literature, parents and teachers would attempt to instruct the younger members of the community in the skills and observations needed to get along in everyday life. Wisdom literature told them what to say or do in a given situation to gain favor with other people.

Most of us are familiar with Aesop's *Fables*. In a way, this was a type of wisdom literature. The moral of the story was instructional—it conveyed a popular truth to the reader. The story was simply a vehicle for the moral, the message to be remembered and taken to heart.

All of us are familiar with the timeworn proverbs of our culture. They also serve to illustrate the purpose of wisdom literature. Most of us could recite a number of proverbs, such as the sage advice: "A fool and his money are soon parted." Some people in this world are careless enough with their money to make this statement true.

The object of this (or any) proverb is to share the *results* of experience with others in order that they might not have to suffer the same painful experience to learn the same idea. The experience is encapsulated in a phrase, and the phrase is passed down from generation to generation, perhaps with an admonition to be careful with your money.

Or, consider the proverb: "A friend in need is a friend indeed." Most of us have experienced false friendship—a relationship in which a person was kind to us or stood by us until trouble came along. Then that person deserted us. This situation is stated in a short phrase, and then passed down from the elders to the younger and less-experienced members of society. If misfortune arises and their friends stand by them, they know that their friendships are true. Why? Collective human experience says so.

To some extent at least, the wisdom literature of the Hebrews served the same purpose. The experience of previous generations could be shared with the younger members of the community, without their having to undergo the same mistakes.

But there was a difference between the general wisdom collections of the various Near Eastern countries and that of the Israelites. Many of the Israelite maxims were based upon the faith of the people, and their deep and abiding trust in Yahweh. Belief in God gave a different emphasis to common sense. Granted, not all of the wisdom literature was so nobly based upon religious ideals. Allowances were made as the collections grew and covered the broader spectrum of Israelite life. But, in general, this belief in Yahweh was certainly an undercurrent in the Israelite wisdom tradition.

In many ways, the wisdom literature of Israel was rather simplistic. The solutions posed fit only specific circumstances. There were only two types of people portrayed: the wise and the foolish. There was no middle ground, and there seemed to be little possibility for advancement.

Traditionally, the wisdom books of the Old Testament include Psalms, Proverbs, Job, Ecclesiastes, Wisdom, Song of Songs, and Sirach. They treat many of the major questions of Israelite life. They also consider major theological questions, especially in the cases of Job and Ecclesiastes.

CLASS ACTIVITY:

Have each student make a list of several contemporary proverbs. Then have the students gather into groups of five or six students and compare their lists. For discussion:

1) Explain the main idea behind each proverb.

2) Why would such proverbs be a kind of wisdom literature?

RESEARCH PROJECT:

Benjamin Franklin was a founding father of the United States. Among his many interests was publishing. Prepare a report on his publishing activity, his involvement with wisdom literature, and the influence his publishing had on the new nation.

PSALMS

Reading: Psalms 2, 29, 51, 119, 122, 137, 150.

Key Idea: A lyrical approach to events in the Old Testament.

The Book of Psalms is a collection of 150 lyrics. It would be more accurate to say, perhaps, that Psalms is a "collection of collections," since smaller collections of these hymns predate the final edition as we have it today.

Some claim that if the entire Old Testament had been lost through some great tragedy, it could be virtually recreated from the Book of Psalms. That's not exactly accurate, since the psalms consider only a few of the major Old Testament themes. It's more accurate to say that the psalms are dependent upon the Old Testament for a lot of their meaning; that is, if we are familiar with the Old Testament, we will have a much better understanding of the psalms.

At the same time, the psalms do speak to a wide range of human emotions and experience. It is this timeless quality that makes the psalms meaningful as prayer to many people today.

The psalms are lyrics—the words to songs. They were intended to be sung rather than read. Perhaps we miss a lot of their meaning when we *read* them, since we know from our own experience that music can color a person's mood and perception.

The psalms were generally attributed to David, and tradition has it that David was a poet and musician, as well as a king. Yet, for one man to write psalms that reflect so much of the Israelite experience (including the period of time long after David) is virtually impossible. We must remember that authorship in the Old Testament was a rather broad idea.

There are several types of psalms in the Old Testament. The psalms can be grouped in different ways. Perhaps one of the clearer ways is to group them by intent. Thus, there are hymns of praise, whose intent is simply to praise Yahweh for the wonders he has done. These psalms often invite the reader (or *listener,* if they are sung), to join in this praise.

Another type are the psalms of lament. These works might show the author's bitterness over a specific situation, or sorrow for some particular reason. Then, the psalm would turn the thought of the hearer to Yahweh and what he could do to help the situation.

Psalms of thanksgiving seem rather obvious, but it should be noted that they occur on both the individual and the national level, depending upon whether the favor received was personal or for everyone.

Psalms of petition ask Yahweh to step into a given situation and do something specific to save his people. Again, these are either individual or national.

Didactic psalms are psalms that teach. They encapsulate the tribal history of Israel in lyrical form, since history could be remembered more easily that way in an age in which people didn't read or write.

Why were songs used to convey ideas? What reasons did the Israelites have for putting their history into musical form?

A song has several built-in memory devices. It uses the characteristics of rhyme, rhythm, and meter. It has a catchy tune that "sticks" in the memory. All these devices working together aid the memory in retaining the message. These devices give a clue as to which word or idea or sound comes next. They form a pattern that the memory retains more easily.

Many people learn their alphabet by learning a song. The song attempts to rhyme the sound of some of the letters, giving the memory clues as to what comes next. It uses a melody to retain interest.

The use of song has its disadvantages, however. Because of the necessity of carrying out the meter or the rhyme, the singer or poet or lyricist occasionally has to "force" a word or idea to keep the pattern intact. This practice is called poetic license, and it can create problems of accuracy. That is why it was stated earlier that we can better understand the psalms if we are familiar with the Old Testament piety that wrote them. The psalms cannot take the place of the Old Testament, but they do reflect it.

The psalms are numbered many different ways. The reasons are numerous, and perhaps not too important for us. We'll follow the enumeration of *The Jerusalem Bible*.

By looking at some of the psalms, we'll be able to discover some of their characteristics. The student should sample the diversity of this (and, indeed, every) biblical book over an extended period of time. The suggested readings for this section display this diversity.

One of the characteristics of lyrics and poetry is that of parallel construction. In one of its more common forms, parallelism expresses the same idea twice, using different words. This is exemplified with great regularity in the psalms, and rather notably in Psalm 2. Most of the verses in this psalm express the same basic thought twice, though not quite in the same way. If we look at verses 3, 4, and 5, we can see this clearly.

> 3 "Now let us break their fetters!
>   Now let us throw off their yoke!"
> 4 The One whose throne is in heaven sits laughing,
>   Yahweh derides them.
> 5 Then angrily he addresses them,
>   In a rage he strikes them with panic. . . .

Note that in each verse, the second part of the line conveys the same idea as the first part, but it uses different words in doing so. This is a memory device that would help the singer remember all the words. Much of our modern music is constructed in the same way.

Not all of the psalms are of Hebrew origin. Most biblical commentators believe that Psalm 29 was originally a Canaanite psalm to their god, Baal. It describes the majesty of a thunderstorm. The Israelites probably took this psalm and changed the name "Baal" to "Yahweh," and then incorporated the psalm into their collection. As we read this psalm, it's easy to visualize the power of a thunderstorm rising in awesome form over Israel.

The first verse of Psalm 51 has a special purpose, as does the opening verse of many of the psalms. Often, the first verse gives directions to the singer on how to perform the psalm. Or, perhaps, this verse gives some historical background for the psalm, as it does in this case. This is one of the five penitential psalms, and is supposedly from the time of David and his sin with Bathsheba. Although the psalm begins by lamenting the author's sinfulness and showing his personal sorrow, it ends on a rather hopeful note.

One of the didactic (teaching) psalms is Psalm 119. Its purpose was to teach the value of the Law of the Lord.

It is quite lengthy, and thus employs another memory device. The format of the psalm is based upon the order of letters in the Hebrew alphabet, and would be quite similar to writing a contemporary poem and beginning each verse with a successive letter of our alphabet. By calling to mind which letter came next in order, the person reciting or singing could usually remember the verse.

During the time after Solomon's reign, the people of the southern kingdom were encouraged rather strongly to worship only at the Temple in Jerusalem. This "unity of sanctuary" provided for a uniform religious experience for the people. But it had the additional political advantage of unifying the country, since periodically everyone had to travel to Jerusalem to worship.

Many of the people would come in caravans, and some of the songs of the Book of Psalms reflect these pilgrimages. We often find in the first verse of many psalms the words, "a song of ascents." These were songs to be sung by the pilgrims on their way up to Jerusalem. Psalm 122 is such a psalm, and it shows the psalmist's joy as his goal was attained:

> How I rejoiced when they said to me,
> "Let us go to the house of Yahweh!"
> And now our feet are standing
> in your gateways, Jerusalem (Ps 122:1-2).

But other psalms are not so joyous. If we look at Psalm 137, for example, we can see the bitterness of the exile in Babylon as the psalmist remembered Jerusalem's former glory. This is one of the saddest songs in the entire Old Testament.

Beside the streams of Babylon
we sat and wept
at the memory of Zion,
leaving our harps
hanging on the poplars there. . . .

How could we sing
one of Yahweh's hymns
in a pagan country?
Jerusalem, if I forget you,
may my right hand wither! (Ps 137:1-5).

The final psalm, 150, is a general hymn of praise that attempts to sum up the entire collection. The first and last words are "alleluia," a Hebrew phrase that means "Praise Yahweh!" This psalm gives us a general indication of the instruments used in the service of the Temple: trumpet, lyre, harp, stringed instruments, pipe, and cymbals. Even dancing (v. 4) was allowed.

We can easily overlook the importance of this book, or glance at it with only a passing interest. In doing so we would fail to recognize its importance in reflecting the faith of Israel. We should not go to the other extreme, however, and see the psalms as more than they really are, that is, a reflection of belief and piety in the Old Testament.

ASSIGNMENT:

The psalms were the popular religious songs of the Hebrew people. In many ways, they parallel contemporary music.

Many of the values and ideas found in the psalms are found in current religious and popular music, because the values in these psalms are so universal. Name a modern religious or popular song that deals with each of the following themes. Now find an Old Testament psalm that treats each of these themes as well.

trust	need	sorrow
glory of God	forgiveness	goodness
gratitude/thanks-giving	nature	love

ECCLESIASTES

Reading: Ecclesiastes 1-3, 6, 11-12.

Key Idea: Life without God is meaningless.

What is it that really makes us happy? Or, perhaps more realistically, what do we *think* would make us happy? Would it be wealth? What about power? Maybe wisdom? What if we tried all of these, and were still unhappy? What lesson could we learn from that? Addressing such questions is the idea behind the Book of Ecclesiastes.

The author, Qoheleth, claimed to be Solomon. But this was likely a literary device on the part of the author to ensure that his writings would be heeded. Qoheleth, the main character of the book, wanted to ask himself the above-mentioned questions, and find out for himself just what would make him happy.

In chapter 2, he tells about his pursuit of pleasure. The text relates how he built numerous monumental works; he acquired slaves, flocks, and even male and female singers. He denied himself nothing. But when he looked at all of his acquisitions, his only real worry was who would get all of his possessions after he was gone!

What about the value of trying to live a good life? Qoheleth looked about, as we all have, and saw good people suffering and evil people prospering. What was the point of trying to do good? Indeed, Qoheleth added, the lot of man and beast was the same. Why should man try to live a good life?

> Both go to the same place; both originate from the dust and to the dust both return. Who knows if the spirit of man mounts upward or if the spirit of the beast goes down to the earth?
>
> I see there is no happiness for man but to be happy in his work, for this is the lot assigned him. Who then can bring him to see what is to happen after his time? (Eccl 3:20-22).

If you're beginning to get the impression that Qoheleth was a rather bitter and cynical man, you're substantially correct. In chapter 6, he laments his own personal fate, as well as that of all humanity. A man could work all of his life and never have the benefit of his possessions; he would die, and they would go to someone else. "All things are vanity, and a chasing of the wind," he proclaimed.

The book offers other examples of the futility of the human condition. In the final two chapters, Qoheleth considered the advantages of youth over old age.

> However great the number of the years a man may live,
> let him enjoy them all, and yet remember that dark days
> will be many (Eccl 11:8).

He seems to be questioning the purpose of life: We're born, we get old, we die. That's about all there is to it. We might as well have a bit of happiness—the "eat, drink, and be merry for tomorrow we die" philosophy echoed elsewhere in the book.

In the final chapter, Qoheleth describes in poetic fashion a human life rushing to its conclusion.

> . . . before the dust returns to the earth as it once came
> from it, and the breath to God who gave it.
>
> Vanity of vanities, Qoheleth says. All is vanity (Eccl
> 12:7-8).

A depressing book? Yes, but not a book without value. If we're not careful, we can easily overlook verse 13 of the last chapter:

> To sum up the whole matter: fear God, and keep his
> commandments, since this is the whole duty of man . . .
> (Eccl 12:13).

God does make a difference in our lives. Life without God is meaningless, and only God can give meaning to the statements of Qoheleth about his pursuit of happiness.

We live in a rather self-centered age. We are urged to serve ourselves, to buy products that will give us status or pleasure. Yet, like Qoheleth, we find that we are still looking for happiness. Part of the difficulty is that a person is more than a material being; a person is a spiritual-material reality. How can that which is only material possibly satisfy anyone? We need those other elements of life that go beyond the material: We need friendships, the love of other people, the love of God.

Qoheleth's book is remarkably contemporary, since it asks many of the same questions that people today ask about life. His conclusion—that we need God—is about the only conclusion we can accept today, if we stop and think about what Qoheleth said.

DISCUSSION:

Qoheleth tried everything in order to find out what gave his life meaning. What are your own ideas about the meaning and values of life—what's important to you? Complete the following statements, and discuss them with others in your class.

1. I think I would be a lot happier if

_____

_____

_____

2. The one thing that bothers me most in life is

_____

_____

_____

3. If I could have all the money I wanted, I would

_____

_____

_____

4. In my life, I'm happiest about

---

5. As I get older, I think I would like to

What do you think Qoheleth would say about your answers?

JOB

Reading: Job 1-2, 38-42.

Key Idea: We have to let God be God.

People often wonder why they have to suffer. Indeed, suffering is one of the greatest of life's mysteries. The Hebrews didn't escape such problems either, and they wrote their reflections on suffering and evil into the Book of Job.

Job is one of the more important books in the Israelite wisdom collection, but it is not often understood. The original story, which was quite brief, is reflected in the suggested readings above. The remainder of the book, a long insertion, was probably added to the original story later on.

Initially, the story was quite simple: Once upon a time, there was a good man named Job who had everything a man could desire. He lost it all, but he kept his faith in God. Subsequently, everything was restored to him.

Later on, the story was applied to the problem of evil and suffering. Many commentators believe that the cycles of speeches from chapters 3 through 37 were inserted at this point. We can divide the book into its three sections rather easily: the original beginning, the insertion of the speeches, and the original ending.

The story began with a description of Job as a good and prosperous man from the land of Uz. He had many possessions, but was truly generous and religious. He tried hard to avoid sin. Through several misfortunes, Job lost everything; his goods were stolen, his children perished, and his servants were killed. Job's response to all these events was:

> "Yahweh gave, Yahweh has taken back.
> Blessed be the name of Yahweh!"
> In all this misfortune Job committed no sin nor offered any insult to God (Jb 1:21-22).

But Job's troubles were only beginning. He was afflicted with a loathsome disease. Even his wife turned away from him, saying that it was foolish to claim that he was innocent of sin. After all, why else would he be suffering, except in punishment for his sins? His response to her was:

"If we take happiness from God's hand, must we not take sorrow too?" And in all this misfortune, Job uttered no sinful word (Jb 2:10).

Anyone who speaks of the "patience of Job" probably never read the text. At this point, the insertion begins and the author has Job complaining loudly over his situation. Job's three friends approached him and, in their speeches to him, demonstrated the traditional Israelite responses to the problem of evil. The general implication of his friends' arguments was that Job had sinned, and he'd better admit it and be sorry. All the while, Job clung to his innocence.

Israelite belief saw evil as a punishment for sin. The purpose of this section of the book is to show that the traditional explanations of the suffering of mankind were terribly inadequate. Job had not sinned, but he was experiencing a great deal of suffering. Finally, Job could take it no longer, and he demanded an explanation from God himself.

The last four chapters show God's interesting answer to Job's demands. He didn't answer Job directly; instead, he reminded Job of his almighty power.

God began by questioning Job's importance. He asked Job where he was during creation. What did Job know about the building of the earth? How was it determined how far upon the shore the ocean could go? What did Job know about the storehouse of the wind or the snow? Who took care of the needs of all the wild animals?

Job recognized what God was doing, and tried to retreat, but God wouldn't let him. He told Job of more of his powers, concerns, and responsibilities. Job responded in humility:

> I have been holding forth on matters I cannot understand,
>   on marvels beyond me and my knowledge. . . .
> I retract all that I have said,
>   and in dust and ashes I repent (Jb 42:3-6).

The point is that we have to let God be God. He owes us nothing, including explanations. Surely, there is some reason for the sufferings we endure. Somehow, it is a part of God's plan. We, like Job, cannot understand it. But that doesn't lessen God's love or concern for us. We really can't understand God's love either, can we? We cannot always demand answers. Even if we knew the reason for suffering, that knowledge wouldn't take the suffering away.

The book concludes with Job being restored to prosperity. The author attempted to answer the problem of suffering, and did so better than anyone else in the Old Testament. Somehow, in God's plan, there is a reason for suffering. But for the person with faith, the goodness and mercy of God will eventually win out.

MORE ON SUFFERING AND EVIL:

People have always wondered about the problem of evil and suffering in this life. Some people seem to have more than their share of problems, but everyone suffers in some way: physical pain, emotional trauma, mental illness, the hurt of misunderstanding, and many other forms.

1) Pinpoint a personal experience that caused you suffering. How did you handle this experience? What were the positive results of the experience? What were the negative results?

2) Did you learn anything from this experience of suffering that will help you deal with suffering and pain in the future?

3) Imagine a situation in which one of your close friends has experienced a personal tragedy and is experiencing a great deal of suffering. What would you say to that friend? What do you think Job would say?

SIRACH

Reading: Foreword, 2-3, 6-7, 26, 30.

Key Idea: The passing on of wisdom from generation to generation.

The Book of Sirach is rather unusual in one respect: We know specifically who wrote it. The text tells us that a man named Jesus son of Eleazar son of Sirach wrote it in the late 100s B.C. His grandson, who is not named in the text, later translated the book and wrote the Foreword.

This book is often called "Ecclesiasticus," because it was used so much by the early church, and was often called the *Liber Ecclesiasticus,* or "church book." Even today we often use this book in our liturgy.

There is little coherence or logical order in the book; it seems to be a catchall of wisdom ideas. It gives both practical and religious advice, lists man's duties toward God, gives general rules for the raising of children, and even tells the reader how to get along in society. The chapters we have read give a general sampling of the text.

The Foreword contains a valuable insight into the difficulties of working with the Bible.

> . . . you will find on examination that the Law itself, the Prophets and the other books differ considerably in translation from what appears in the original text (Sir, Foreword 24-26).

We begin to see the religious side of the author in chapter 2, where he lists man's duties toward God. His basic idea is the necessity of trust in God, as proven by the collective experience of mankind. Thus, Sirach could write:

> Look at the generations of old and see:
> who ever trusted in the Lord and was put to shame? (Sir 2:10-11).

Chapter 3 shows duties toward parents. Perhaps many people misunderstand this section, just as they misunderstand the fourth commandment. The Israelites had few (if any) commandments for children. Besides, it's easy to respect your parents when you are young; they can do so much more than you can do. But this passage, like the fourth commandment, actually deals with adults and *their* parents. In short, it deals with what our responsibilities are to our parents when we are *both* older.

> My son, support your father in his old age,
>   do not grieve him during his life.
> Even if his mind should fail, show him sympathy, . . .
>   for kindness to a father shall not be forgotten . . .
>   like frost in sunshine, your sins will melt away (Sir 3:12-15).

Each of us knows the importance of both having a friend and being a friend to others. When all else fails, friendship can be a truly wonderful experience. Yet, we must be cautious in choosing our friends, since so much is at stake.

These ideas are found in Sirach's poem on friendship (6:5-17). He first lists the various kinds of friends, and tells how one can be certain of another's friendship. Ideally, we not only have friends; we are friends to others as well. Sirach's poem thus offers us some ideas about what that entails.

Chapter 7 lists a series of principles for a person in public life. However, these principles are general enough to fit anyone's situation and, in that sense, they are valid for us today. The chapter also speaks of family duties and other general topics, and thus gives us some clues about values in Old Testament times.

Largely because of the culture in which they lived, the attitude of the writers of the Old Testament seems rather harsh toward women, at least by today's standards. Yet, there are passages that exalt womanhood, such as Sirach 26:1-4, 13-18. These lines extol the ideal woman and set up a series of standards for Israelite women to follow in their own lives.

Chapter 30 gives guidelines for the raising of children, and shows us the results of accomplishing this task successfully.

> Even when the father dies, he might well not be dead,
> since he leaves his likeness behind him.
> In life he has had the joy of his company,
> dying, he has no anxieties (Sir 30:4-5).

Much of the remainder of the chapter is concerned with the necessity of discipline, especially for young people. It points out an old familiar belief: "Spare the rod and spoil the child."

Human nature hasn't changed much over the years. In that fact lies the value of the wisdom books. The authors took the collective wisdom of previous ages and passed it down to generations still to come, with the certainty that their advice would remain valid.

> Instruction in wisdom and knowledge
> had been committed to writing in this book
> by Jesus son of Sira, Eleazar, of Jerusalem,
> who has rained down wisdom from his heart.
> Happy is he who busies himself with these things,
> and grows wise by taking them to heart (Sir 50:27-30).

DISCUSSION:

The authors of the Old Testament seem to have little to say about the status of women, largely because of the culture in which they lived. As we have seen, however, the author of Sirach/Ecclesiasticus made some remarkable statements for the times about women (Sir 26:1-4, 13-18).

Gather into groups of five or six students and read Proverbs 31:10-31. What are the main values the author is expressing concerning women? How are these values applicable to women in contemporary society?

WISDOM

Reading: Wisdom 3, 4, 6.

Key Idea: Short sermons about the problems of life.

Our final look into the wisdom literature will be directed at the Book of Wisdom itself. It might surprise us that this book was written at Alexandria in Egypt, rather than in Palestine. Since the time of the Exile, several large colonies of Jews had settled at various places, with a particularly large settlement in certain areas of Egypt. This book, written sometime around 100-50 B.C., developed somewhat outside the mainstream of Jewish thought, and was largely influenced by Greek ideas prevalent in Egypt at this time.

The author never actually claimed to be Solomon, but several general hints give the reader this idea. Clearly, Solomon was not involved in a book that appeared as late as this one, and this technique, as we have seen before, was a literary device employed by authors to gain acceptance of their work.

The purpose of the author was somewhat different from the other wisdom writers. The others wanted to pass wisdom and experience down from age to age. They wrote primarily for the instruction of youth. But the author of the Book of Wisdom was writing more for his contemporaries who had become somewhat lax in their Jewish faith and heritage. Some had begun to place so much emphasis on the Greek ideas and philosophies prevalent at this time, that they were overlooking some of the more important ideas of their own tradition.

Unlike many other wisdom books, the Wisdom of Solomon does not use short proverbs or catchy sayings to make its point. It uses whole paragraphs, or even short sermons, to treat the issues of death and suffering, judgment, and the importance of seeking wisdom in the religious sense.

In the Old Testament, wisdom wasn't just intellectual ability, although that was involved. It also included the idea of how man was to live his life—what specific decisions he had to make. While wisdom was to be sought, it was also seen as a gift of God, and sometimes it was even personified, and found residing with God.

The readings for this section point out some of the more generally used readings from the Book of Wisdom. In chapter 3, we find the author's advice to the reader as to the real meaning behind death. While this section is not terribly specific, it seems to indicate in a general way belief in the individual soul. This was one of the Greek ideas that was appropriated by the author for this work. The passage mentions how those who have been faithful will be protected and cared for by God, and how those who were evil shall be punished. This is possibly the first time this general idea, on a personal level, at least, is found in the Scriptures. Obviously, we cannot take one text too far, but we find here the possible beginnings of belief in individual immortality and judgment.

> But the souls of the virtuous are in the hands of God. . . .
> In the eyes of the unwise, they did appear to die, . . .
> but they are in peace.
> If they experienced punishment as men see it,
> their hope was rich with immortality (Wis 3:1-4).

What about a person who died at an early age? How did the wisdom writers give meaning to apparent tragedy? It was expected that a person would live to the fullness of years. What if that person died before his or her time? The author responded to this problem also.

> The virtuous man, though he die before his time, will find rest.
> Length of days is not what makes age honorable,
> nor number of years the true measure of life. . . .
> He has sought to please God, so God has loved him. . . .
> He has been carried off so that evil may not warp his understanding
> or treachery seduce his soul (Wis 4:7-11).

The author reminds us of a beautiful truth: that age is not the real criterion for success in life. Other elements are far more important. If we love the Lord and love one another, we have achieved what the Lord asked us to do. The amount of time it takes—short or long—really doesn't matter. The author seems to describe a person who was so good that God took him to himself, lest the person be immersed in the wickedness of the world.

Lines such as these will not solve our problems about early death. But they do remind us that God has a plan that we do not understand, and that somehow he will work out everything for those who love him.

The sixth chapter of the book is a challenge to the reader to seek wisdom in all that is done, since it is a gift of God and thus something desirable.

Wisdom is bright, and does not grow dim.
By those who love her she is readily seen,
and found by those who look for her (Wis 6:12).

The remainder of the book can be divided into two sections. The first shows the author's appreciation of wisdom and how he sought it. The second gives the reason for seeking wisdom: *because of God's care and goodness in watching over his people, particularly in past experiences such as the Exodus.*

This brief look at the wisdom literature has given us the opportunity to sample this unusual style of biblical writing. But, more importantly, it has shown us the timeless quality of the Bible as the word of God.

CHAPTER SUMMARY:

1. The major purpose of the wisdom literature was to pass down the prevailing wisdom of one age to another.

2. The wisdom collection of Israel was based largely on the faith of the people in Yahweh.

3. The Psalms were a collection of the lyrics of songs, and reflect much of the belief of the people of the Old Testament.

4. Psalms were used to convey ideas because they utilized memory devices, and few of the Hebrews could read or write.

5. Qoheleth reminded his readers that life without God was meaningless.

6. Job told his readers that we have to let God be God.

7. Wisdom literature was used not only for the instruction of youth, but also to remind the Jews outside Palestine of their heritage and their beliefs.

CHAPTER FIVE IN REVIEW:

1. What was the basic purpose of the Israelite wisdom literature?

2. How did the writers of the wisdom literature accomplish their purpose?

3. Why did songs and poems form such a sizeable part of the Old Testament?

4. In what sense is Ecclesiastes a contemporary book?

5. Why were the traditional explanations of evil, as found in the Book of Job, considered inadequate by Job's author?

6. Why was a large part of the wisdom literature seemingly interested in the "non-religious" aspect of Israelite life?

TERMS TO KNOW:

wisdom	Qoheleth	proverb
parallelism	maxim	literary device
lyric	cynic	psalm
contemporary		

SPECIAL PROJECT:

What do you think are the characteristics of a wise person? Is it age? Experience? Interview at least four people from different age groups, gathering their opinions on wisdom.

What were their responses? Share them with the class.

6

From the Exile to the New Testament

The section of the Old Testament that we will consider next covers a period of over 500 years, but it provides us with very little information about that period. Largely because of the disarray of the country after the exile, and also because of Greek and Roman domination, the people were too busy with the day-to-day business of survival to keep many records. The writings that remain from this period show some further growth and development in Judaism as it moved toward New Testament times. After we look at a few specific books from this period, we'll consider some of the religious institutions and situations in Israel that will prepare us to understand better the background for the New Testament.

EZRA / NEHEMIAH

Reading: Ezra 1, 4, 7, 9, 10.

Key Idea: The problems of the restoration in the Promised Land.

The exile of the Jewish people to Babylon was difficult, but eventually, the Babylonian empire fell to the Persians and the Medes. The Persians were generally rather well-disposed toward captured na-

141

tions, although they could become harsh if the captives got out of line.

In 538 B.C., Cyrus, the king of Persia, issued a decree (see Ezra 1) freeing the Hebrews from Babylon. In this decree, he also agreed to fund the restoration of the Temple in Jerusalem.

Two important Israelites figured significantly in this period. Ezra, the champion of religious purity and reform, restored the ideal of Jewish law. Nehemiah, the governor, was to rebuild the walls of the city of Jerusalem.

The books of Ezra and Nehemiah are two of the best sources for information about the period after the exile. Yet, these two books, in their present state, at least, are quite out of order chronologically. The text is confusing, and it's difficult for the reader to determine the correct order of events. Historically, Nehemiah probably came first, although both are roughly from the same period.

To understand the difficulty of the task facing Ezra and Nehemiah, the reader must imagine what it would be like to physically move about one-third to one-half of a nation's population into exile for about 60 years. We can only wonder how land and property disputes were settled, and how the people picked up the pieces of their past traditions when they returned. It was also partially because of the confusion of this period that some of the Old Testament books were put into writing. There was no certainty that the People of God would remain cohesive during the exile, and so many traditions were written down to preserve them.

Nehemiah's greatest contribution as governor (see Nehemiah 2) was to rebuild the fallen walls of Jerusalem. The size of the rebuilt walls didn't really matter; after 60 years of enslavement, the walls had become a symbol of autonomy. The book of Nehemiah relates the difficulties surrounding this reconstruction.

During the time of Ezra, the rebuilding of the Temple was begun at Persian expense. The Temple of Solomon had been destroyed in the siege of Jerusalem in 587 B.C. After a short time, however, construction on the new Temple was halted by outside interference (see Ezra 4). There seemed to be some dispute among the Persian rulers after Cyrus as to whether or not the Persians had actually agreed to fund this project.

In 521 B.C., Darius I had become king of Persia. He was questioned about the Temple issue, and so he looked up the original decree of Cyrus in the royal archives (see Ezra 6). With the issue settled in the Israelites' favor, the Temple reconstruction was continued, and it was completed in 515 B.C.

Ezra, as a religious reformer and leader of the people, was aware that in a time of turmoil such as this, only a strong adherence to the Law could keep the small, struggling nation together. His zealous insistence upon religious purity seems somewhat strange and terribly exclusive by our standards today. But he believed that it was the only way the Jewish nation would survive.

Chapters 9 and 10 of Ezra show the harsh measures necessary to preserve Judaism at this time. The people had mingled with and intermarried people from other nations. While this had been a forbidden practice in earlier times, religious tradition had suffered during the exile.

At Ezra's urging, the people agreed to keep away from foreign nations, and even to repudiate their foreign wives and children born of them. The book concludes with a list of people who had married foreign women, and then it tells us:

> All these had married foreign wives; they put them
> away, both women and children (Ezr 10:44).

While these practices seem unthinkable today, we have to be aware of the situation at the time. Judaism was emerging from bondage in Babylon, and only the sternest measures could keep it alive; or, at least, these measures could keep Judaism undiluted by the cultures and beliefs that surrounded it.

The new Temple that had been built was a disappointment to many. It lacked the grandeur of the Temple of Solomon. But at least it was something to remind the people that their God remained in their midst.

It was the same with the reconstructed walls in Jerusalem. Any serious effort by a major foe would have been successful in breaching the walls. That wasn't the point. The reconstructed walls were a symbol of independence and, thus, a symbol of national identity.

Through his prophets Yahweh had promised to bring his people back to Israel. He had done so. But the crucible of the exile had refined Judaism and formed it in a different mold. From this point on, the Jews became the people of the Torah—the great book of the Law.

DISCUSSION:

Break the class into four groups. Each group should discuss one of the following scenarios.

The period immediately after the exile must have been chaotic.

1) You are the head of a family with several young children. What are the first things you must concern yourself with as you return to your homeland? Remember the exile lasted about 60 years.

2) You are a religious or a political leader. What are the first things you must see to?

3) You are a young person, unmarried and still living with your parents, but you want to get married. What do you think your responsibilities are?

4) You are old and your family is grown. You went into exile as a very young child. What lies ahead for you?

After your discussions come together as a class and compare your findings. Where is God and the covenant in the priorities you have just established?

1 AND 2 MACCABEES

Reading: 1 Maccabees 1, 2, 6.
          2 Maccabees 7, 12.

Key Idea: Loyalty to Yahweh in time of persecution.

The persecution of individuals for their religious beliefs has taken many forms. Some forms are rather subtle, and some are quite obvious. The books of Maccabees relate one of the more strenuous persecutions of the Jewish people in Old Testament times.

Alexander the Great had conquered the empire of the Persians, and he died in 323 B.C. His empire was divided up among his officers, one of whom was named Seleucus. He ruled over what remained of the Greek and Babylonian portion of Alexander's empire. This area included Palestine, and during the time of the books of Maccabees, the area was ruled by descendants of Seleucus.

The most notable of those descendants was Antiochus IV, who began to rule around 175 B.C. After a brief and successful campaign against Egypt, he entered Palestine and began a rather systematic persecution of the Jews.

The two books of Maccabees relate some of the history and theology of this period (175-135 B.C.). But like many other books in the Old Testament, their purpose is not just to report straight history. The authors wanted to theologize on that history; to reflect upon it and find its meaning, to see what God had done for them.

The reader can sample nearly any selection from these two books, and will find story after story about persecution. Our selected readings show rather clearly the tremendous suffering the Jews endured under Antiochus. However, the reader will discover quickly that the enemy was not really the Seleucid rulers, but rather the Jews who succumbed to the pressure of persecution and abandoned their beliefs. The books attempt to show, during a time of national trial, how important faithfulness to Yahweh really was. The people had been chosen by God and formed as a nation; those benefits imposed the obligation of fidelity.

> . . . The king appointed inspectors for the whole people and directed all the towns of Judah to offer sacrifice one after another. Many of the people—that is, every apostate from the Law—rallied to them, and so committed evil in the country, forcing Israel into hiding in all their places of refuge (1 Mc 1:51-53).

Antiochus' actions gradually precipitated a revolt, led first by Mattathias. He was an elderly priest, and the father of five sons. Their rebellion met with some initial success, and an increasing number of followers joined them. When Mattathias died of old age, he named his son Simeon as father of the family, and his son Judas as head of the army of rebellion.

The next several chapters show some of the military victories gained by the small army, and chapter 6 tells of the eventual death of the ruler, Antiochus.

Through this rebellion, which is now called the Maccabean revolt, Israel actually gained a sort of independence for a few decades. Eventually, the nation would fall to one of the greatest empires known to history, the Romans, but that was still decades away.

The formation of the theological ideas of this period was even more important than the Israelites' temporary independence. In 2 Maccabees 7, we find the rather grotesque account of the martyrdom of a Jewish mother and her seven sons. They all chose to die, rather than to violate some of the laws of their ancestors. The interesting point is that, as each son died, he uttered a statement relevant to belief in life after death. We can find the beginnings of belief in reward of the good, punishment of the evil, and even resurrection of the body in these statements.

We find another important idea in the Second Book of Maccabees, chapter 12. Judas and his men fought a battle in which several of his men were killed. Judas prayed that the sins of the dead men might be "blotted out" (see v. 42). Then they took up a collection and sent it off to Jerusalem so that an expiatory sacrifice might be offered.

The author reminds us that

> . . . If he had not expected the fallen to rise again it would have been superfluous and foolish to pray for the dead, whereas if he had in view the splendid recompense reserved for those who make a pious end, the thought was holy and devout. This was why he had this atonement sacrifice offered for the dead, so that they might be released from their sin (2 Mc 12:44-46).

No single text can be used to support such a broad idea as immortality or resurrection, but it can furnish us with general indications of what some of the people believed.

These books showed the Jewish community that faithfulness to God, even in time of persecution, was essential. The greatest enemies were not those from outside the community, but rather from within—those who would forsake their faith.

FOR REFLECTION:

We have seen that the Jews suffered greatly under the rule of Antiochus. Think of other instances throughout history when a people suffered greatly for what they believed in.

Write a short essay on what beliefs you are willing to suffer for. In your essay deal with things that are concrete and real in your life. For example, are you willing to tell your friends that you will not sneak into a movie or a concert, or that you are not willing to pick up a few items in a store and "forget" to pay for them? Are you willing to say no when everyone else says yes? Will you abide by your beliefs even when you know you will be laughed at?

SPECIAL PROJECT:

Using a concordance to the Bible as a reference, trace the concept of immortality through the Old Testament. How did the concept change from the time God called Abraham to the time of the Maccabean revolt?

THE CREATION ACCOUNTS OF GENESIS

Reading: Genesis 1, 2.

Key Idea: The religious truths of the creation accounts.

The reader might wonder why we consider the creation accounts at this point of our study of the Old Testament. Although the origin of the accounts is quite ancient, their writing down took place later. Also, we're now at a point in our study of the Old Testament where we can better understand what the author was trying to say to his people.

It would be unfortunate to read the creation accounts at the beginning of the Book of Genesis (there are two separate accounts), and then dismiss them as an unexplained mystery or a semihistorical curiosity. To do so would be to fail to discover what the author had in mind for his readers: some answers to a view of the whole world. As we study the creation accounts briefly, we will find that their purpose was far more serious than giving an account of the world's origins.

It's really unfortunate that so many people have become embroiled in bitter controversy over some of the more beautiful chapters of the Bible. Yet, that is what often happens when people read these creation accounts.

Most of the difficulty stems from a simple misunderstanding. People seem to forget why they are even reading the Bible. We're not looking for any historical or scientific truth—we're seeking the religious message. That's why the Bible was written. People seem to forget this when they read the fantastic descriptions of creation, and then feel just a bit uncomfortable with the idea that the passages they have just read totally contradict science. We'll see that the creation accounts really don't contradict science if we just ask the right questions.

Many scholars believe that the first several chapters of Genesis came from a different era than the rest of the book. We can best understand the Hebrew accounts of creation if we compare them with the creation accounts of other cultures from the same geographic area. Let's examine a typical account from the ancient Near East first, so that we can see the context in which the Hebrews were writing. There's quite a connection.

A typical account of creation was that of the Babylonians. It was called the *Enuma Elish Epic,* and it was fairly representative as a creation account. In this epic, there were two gods: Marduk, a god of good, and Tiamat, a god of evil. To shorten a rather long and tedious story, Marduk and Tiamat engaged one another in combat, and they struggled in a vast, primordial mess known as chaos. Marduk finally won the struggle, and as he carved up Tiamat, he made the various elements of creation: the earth, the sky, and so on. This accounted for the presence of both good and evil in the world.

Now, take a good look at the first Hebrew account of creation. Remember our main question with the Bible is, "What is the *religious* message?" The Hebrew author was quite likely making an attempt to say to the Babylonians and others that they were quite seriously in error in their very perception of God. They weren't necessarily wrong about creation—that wasn't really the issue. Rather, they were wrong about some basic truths about God himself. Our author didn't know where the world came from any more than did his Near East counterparts. But he was interested in straightening out a few religious ideas that were actually far more important than that of the world's origin.

The very first idea we learn from the Hebrew creation account is that there are not two gods, but rather only one. The Babylonian account, as well as most others, had two gods. One god was good, and the other was evil.

Second, this one God of the Hebrews was good. There was no god of evil, and there was no evil in God.

Third, God made everything. We don't know how he made everything—what all the processes were—but that doesn't matter. God stands behind all creation as its source. His creation was not the violent life-and-death struggle depicted in the *Enuma Elish Epic;* rather, it was effortless. God spoke, and creation occurred.

The fourth idea to be learned is that everything God made was good. We need only look at the depiction of creation to see the author's insistence upon this point. From the fourth day on, each day's work was described by the author as being either "good" or "very good."

The fifth point showed that, since God was good, and since everything he made was good, then evil must have its origins elsewhere. Indeed, that was one of the reasons behind the account of Adam and Eve later on: to show that evil came from humankind, and not from God.

The descriptions of the creation account show the ancient Hebrew view of the universe. The sky was depicted as a large inverted dome, and water was above it. Openings in the dome allowed for the presence of rain. Stars moved across the dome on tracks.

No one today would hold that this is the way the universe really operates. But, lest we feel too superior to our unsophisticated author, we must remember that he relied only upon his eyesight and his imagination. All things considered, he didn't fare too badly. He was unaware of a more scientific explanation of the origins of the world. But his insights into the religious truths believed by his people were far more important. The accounts of creation were written to advance these religious truths, not to give a specific account of the origin of the universe.

EXERCISE:

The Hebrews had to rely on their eyesight and their imagination in forming their creation accounts. Obviously, they had none of to-day's science and technology.

How would you describe creation if you could use only your eyesight and your imagination? What makes the sun move across the sky? Why does it rain or snow? Where does wind come from? What about the stars? How did everything come into being?

Compare your account with the Hebrew account of creation.

THE DIFFERENT GROUPS WITHIN JUDAISM

It is important to be aware of the different groups that had developed within Judaism as the end of Old Testament times approached. All influenced the later New Testament writings, yet they have their roots in the Old Testament. The most important groups were the following:

1. Pharisees

Although the origin of the Pharisees is uncertain, they first appeared before 100 B.C. They were a lay group who placed great emphasis on the Law. They also believed, however, that the oral tradition surrounding the Law was equally binding. This had the effect of giving newer and updated interpretations of the Law.

This was a highly significant group. They gave a direction to Judaism after the Romans destroyed Jerusalem in A.D. 70. Some of the gospel accounts appear to be quite hard on the Pharisees, although this is due more to their hypocrisy than to their religious viewpoint.

2. Sadducees

The Sadducees were a much smaller group than the Pharisees, and they were made up of the conservative priestly and aristocratic classes. They believed in the Law of Moses, the first five books of the Bible, with no further development. Thus, they rejected such Pharisaic beliefs as resurrection, demons, and angels; they probably had little or no belief in a messiah.

3. Essenes

This unusual Jewish group lived in a sort of monastic-like community at Qumran, on the shores of the Dead Sea. They believed themselves to be the "Sons of Light"; all others were God's enemies. In their communal life, they studied the scriptures, held property in common, ate a common meal, and worked at manual labor. They believed in baptism, and had numerous ritual washings and purifications. They were defeated by the Romans in A.D. 70, but not before they hid their most important documents and scriptures in caves. These were discovered in modern times (1947), and were termed the "Dead Sea Scrolls."

4. Zealots

This revolutionary group was dedicated to the overthrow of the Roman government in Palestine. The Zealots were a distinct minority that sometimes used violent means to make their point. They led the rebellion that eventually ended with the defeat of Jerusalem by the Romans in A.D. 70. One of Jesus' disciples (Simon) was a former Zealot.

We have considered God's plan for salvation as this plan began to unfold in the pages of the Old Testament. We have looked both at the theology and the events surrounding this plan. Not every book in the Old Testament was included; the aim of this book is limited to following the main events of the Old Testament. A competent biblical commentary would serve to answer in detail any questions you might have about the Old Testament writings.

In light of the promise God made to Abraham, we saw the formation of the nation of Israel, and also her election by Yahweh. We saw the Israelites enter a land of their own. What remains is the fulfillment of the third part of the promise: Through this land and nation, all the nations of the earth will find blessing. That is the story of the New Testament and of its central figure, Jesus of Nazareth.

CHAPTER SUMMARY:

1. There is little historical information available from the time of the exile to the time of the beginning of the New Testament.

2. Ezra rebuilt the Jewish faith after the exile; Nehemiah restored the walls around Jerusalem, which were a symbol of an independent Jewish nation.

3. Many of the measures used to preserve Judaism after the exile were harsh, but were deemed necessary for Judaism's survival.

4. The Maccabean revolt gave the Jews brief political independence, but also provided theological development of the concept of immortality.

5. The purpose of the creation accounts in Genesis was to reveal truths about God.

6. There were many divergent groups within Judaism toward the close of Old Testament times.

CHAPTER SIX IN REVIEW:

1. What were some of the problems faced by the Hebrews returning from the exile? What were some of the problems of those who had remained in Palestine during the exile?

2. How does the understanding of life after death change in the period of the books of Maccabees from what we have already seen in the Old Testament?

3. What was the purpose behind the Hebrew creation accounts?

4. What are the religious truths we learn from the Hebrew creation accounts?

5. How does our present-day world view differ from that of the ancient Hebrews?

WORDS TO KNOW:

restoration	theology	immortality
persecution	Enuma Elish Epic	Marduk
Tiamat	Pharisee	Sadducee
Essene	Zealot	
contemporary	Torah	

TERMS TO KNOW:

Through research in your school library or through personal interviews, find out about contemporary Judaism. What are some of the differences between the Judaism of the Old Testament and contemporary Judaism?